S I M P L Y
SOUTHERN

Cooking
with
Susan Dale

To Lucy!
Enjoy!
Susan

BY

SUSAN PITTS DALE

Published by Eveready Press
Nashville, Tennessee
Book Design by Melissa Solomon/Eveready Press
Photographers: Jackie Chancey, Brad Mayo, Mimi Mayo, Kevin Nunn and Eveready Staff
ISBN: 978-1-60148-005-7

Dedication

To my son Perry, who loves my cooking.

To my mother Nancy Lee Perkins Pitts,
who taught me so much.

To the memory of my grandmother,
Nancy Kimbrough Perkins, a great cook.

And finally, to all those who have enjoyed my cooking,
and encouraged me to write this book.

Acknowledgements

There are so many people to thank for their help and contributions.

My son, Perry, who has been my taster.

My parents, Nancy Lee and Flip Pitts who have always encouraged me.

My sisters, Neill Pitts, Ellen Mayo, K.K. Rainey and Polly Cullen
for their contributions and editing.

All of my nieces and nephews: Brad Mayo, Mimi Mayo, Anna Mayo,
Caroline Rainey, Bo Rainey and Katye Cullen.
(Mimi and Brad took several of the photos)

Family and friends who have shared their recipes with me: Betty and
Jimmie Perkins, Catharine O'Bryan, Judy Traughber, Pam and
Bobby Chilton, Becky Marshall, Ella Beesley, Jean Crawford,
BeBe Reinhardt, Doris McNew, Judy Harris,
Mary May, and Damon and Mark Rogers.

To those who are no longer with us:
Nana (my grandmother- Nancy K. Perkins),
Bibbie (my great aunt – Louise K. Truett),
Other Mama (my great-grandmother – Lizzie W. Kimbrough),
Barbara Chilton, Big C (Catherine F. Beasley), Jeanne Allen,
Jane McGown, Mrs. Hutton Brown, Sr. and Sam O'Bryan.

Friends who have lent me so much encouragement:
Laura Bearden, Jenny Breeden, Linda Miller, Cassie Winsett,
Maggie Russell, Paula Bennett, Susan Clayton, Lindsay Boyd (my techie),
Carol Wilker, Brenda Williams, Mandy Wachtler, Adam West and
the Nichols Sisters (Jan Smith and Nan Crafton) and so
many other who have helped in many ways.

Finally, my extreme gratitude to the Stevens Family at Eveready Press,
and especially Jadyn Stevens who has led me through this process,
and is wise beyond his years.

Table of Contents

Hors d'oeuvres and Appetizers   3

Soups and Sandwiches   31

Salad and Dressings   51

Eggs, Cheese, Rice and Pasta   79

Vegetables   97

Fish and Seafood   125

Poultry   141

Meat   155

Sauces, Marinades and Gravies   169

Pickles and Preserves   183

Bread and Cakes   191

Cookies and Candy   227

Pies and Other Desserts   237

Beverages   257

Prep Work   265

Suggested Menus   267

Entertaining Journal   275

Family Favorites   283

Measurement Tables   287

Hints   291

Index   295

Foreword

I first wrote this part before I started transcribing the recipes that follow. That was over 2 years ago. Yes, it took me a while, but I did have other things to do like earn a living and raise a son. During the last couple of years I have also picked up more recipes, and developed a few myself.

My son, Perry, has wanted me to open a restaurant for years. I keep telling him how hard running one would be, but he doesn't get it. Who knows, maybe someday I will. At least I know Perry likes my cooking.

For years people have said, "Write a cookbook." So, I guess this is it. I've always been one to share my recipes, and I appreciate others doing the same. What you'll find here are selections from family and friends, and several of my own concoctions. Some of these Southern favorites date back to my great-grandmother.

I have tried to give credit to those who have given me their recipes. I have learned a great deal about cooking from so many, especially my mother and grandmother. There are so many of their dishes here, it would be impossible to credit them every place I need to do so. I have also learned on my own by trial and error.

My family and I prepare food for all sorts of occasions. I have done some catering for friends, and have even incorporated my cooking into my real estate business by having Agents' Open Houses at listings for breakfast, lunch and the cocktail hour. We tailgate for Vanderbilt and the Titans football games. I get together with a group of my high school friends, and we all contribute to the fare. Over the years, our family has had parties at Christmas, for bridal couples, birthdays, and all sorts of other celebrations. Holidays always mean a big meal in which everyone is usually involved during the preparation.

Those who know my family know that we are all very opinionated, which, of course, is not always a good thing. But in preparing food, I feel that there are products that should be used, and others that should not. For instance, mayonnaise means mayonnaise, not salad dressing, and whipping cream means real cream, not whipped topping. I have never been able to figure out what is in that stuff. There are places in some of these recipes where I might use brand names because I have found that these particular products are what I consider the best.

In many cases throughout the book, there are tips following the recipe. There are also places where I tell the way a certain dish came to me, or how it evolved to what it is today.

As we all know, certain foods work well together. Toward the end of this compilation are some suggested menus. I tend to forget what I served when and to whom. So, there is a journal at the end to record the menus and guest lists for parties, as well as a place to list the things that your family likes best. Finally, you'll find measurement tables, and some hints that might help you in the kitchen.

I hope you enjoy this as much as I have enjoyed putting it together. I also hope that all my family, friends, and business associates will be satisfied with this long awaited work.

Appetizers

Appetizers

CHEESE STRAWS

1 stick	Butter (melted)
12 oz.	Extra Sharp Cheddar Cheese (grated)
1 ½ c.	Flour
1 t.	Baking Powder (heaping)
	Cayenne Pepper

Melt butter. Grate cheese in food processor and add to butter. Put dough blade on food processor and add cheese and butter. Add flour and baking powder a little bit at a time. Sprinkle in cayenne pepper to taste. Once mixture is a doughy consistency, place it in a cookie press using either a saw-toothed disc or a star- shaped tip. Press onto a cookie sheet and bake at 375°. Cook 9-10 min. if using the saw-toothed disc, or 12-13 min. with the star-shaped tip, or in either case until the edges start to brown. These can get too brown quickly, so keep an eye on them.

CHEESE DATES, PECANS, OR OLIVES
Using above recipe, take a small amount of dough and roll over a date, pecan or olive. Bake on a cookie sheet at 375° for 12-14 min. until the bottoms begin to brown.

Our recipe for cheese straws has come to be after trying many different ones. These are great to put out for any occasion. They are also great to give to others.

BAKED BRIE EN CROUTE

1 wheel	Brie
1	Egg
1T	Water
	Puff pastry dough

Wrap a wheel of Brie in puff pastry dough, and pinch seams. Mix egg and water. Brush over dough. Place on buttered cookie sheet and bake for 10 minutes at 400°. Then for 20 minutes at 325° until golden brown. Lift off with a spatula, and let stand for a few minutes before serving.

For a different flavor, cook some dried apricots in boiling water and a little sugar until soft. Drain and place on top of the Brie before wrapping it in the dough.

Sister K.K. brought this to our family, and makes it for all of our parties. I make a small one, and use it on a tray with other cheeses, crackers, and fresh fruit.

PINEAPPLE CHEESE BALL

2 – 8oz. pkgs.	Cream Cheese (softened)
8 oz.	Crushed Pineapple (drained)
¼ c.	Chopped Green Bell Pepper
2 c.	Chopped Pecans
2 T.	Finely Grated Onion
1 T.	Season Salt

Save ½ cup of pecans, and mix all other ingredients. Form a ball, and refrigerate. When ball is well chilled, roll in the ½ cup of pecans. Serve with crackers.

This makes a large cheese ball, and can be split in half to make two smaller ones.
If splitting, use more pecans when covering the balls.

HOT ARTICHOKE DIP

1 can	Artichoke Hearts (chopped)
3 T.	Finely Chopped Onion
2/3 c.	Hellmann's Mayonnaise
2/3 c.	Grated Parmesan Cheese
5-6 strips	Cooked Bacon (broken up)
	Cayenne Pepper to taste

Mix all ingredients and bake 20-30 minutes in a casserole dish at 350°. Then broil. Serve with Tricuits.

Most everybody has an artichoke dip recipe. Hope that this will be one that you'll enjoy using.

COLD ARTICHOKE SPREAD

1 can	Artichoke Hearts (chopped)
3	Chopped Hard Boiled Eggs
2/3 c.	Hellmann's Mayonnaise
1 T.	Prepared Mustard
	Cayenne Pepper to Taste
2-3 strips	Cooked and Crumbled Bacon

Mix all ingredients except bacon and chill. Top with bacon when ready to serve.

PAM'S SPINACH SQUARES

2	Eggs (beaten)
1 c.	Flour
1 c.	Milk
1 t.	Seasoned Salt
1 stick	Butter
½ t.	Garlic Salt or Plain Salt
1 10 oz. pkg	Spinach
2 c.	Grated Sharp Cheddar Cheese

Mix eggs, milk, and melted butter. Add flour, seasoned salt, and garlic salt. Drain spinach and add along with grated cheese. Spray a 9x13 baking pan with Pam. Place mixture in pan, and bake at 350° for 30 minutes. Cut in 1 ½ inch squares.

My friend Pam introduced me to this treat. I don't use as much cheese as the original recipe calls for, so you can add more if you like. These make a great side dish for a meal when cut in larger squares. This can be doubled easily in one bowl when you need two recipes. They also freeze well.

CUCUMBER BALL

1 – 8oz. pkg.	Softened Cream Cheese
2 T.	Grated Onion
1	Cucumber -
	peeled, cut up, and drained with seeds removed
½ t.	Garlic Salt
2 T.	Mayonnaise
	Tabasco to taste
	Salt (if needed)

Shape into ball and refrigerate. Spread over crackers.

K.K.'s Spinach Dip

1 10 oz. pkg.	Spinach
1 pkg.	Knorr's Vegetable Soup Mix
1 c.	Sour Cream
½ c.	Hellmann's Mayonnaise
1 can	Water chestnuts (chopped)
3 T	Onion (grated)
	Cayenne Pepper to taste

Thaw and drain spinach. Mix all ingredients. Chill. Serve with crackers.

This recipe is always a favorite! K.K. usually makes it for us.

CREAM CHEESE ROLLS

1 can	Crescent Rolls
1 pkg. (3-4oz.)	Softened Cream Cheese
1 small jar or can	Chopped Mushrooms
	Cayenne Pepper to taste

Mix cream cheese, mushrooms and pepper. Spread some of the mixture on a triangle of the dough, and roll it up. Bake for 12 minutes at 375°. Each recipe makes 8 rolls. Make them smaller by cutting the dough in smaller triangles.

Options to add to cream cheese: grated onion and crumbled bacon; ground ham; crumbled cooked sausage.

BROCCOLI DIP

5 10 oz. boxes	Uncooked Chopped Broccoli (thawed and drained)
5 6 oz.	rolls Garlic Cheese
1 8 oz. can	Mushrooms and Stems
2 cans	Cream of Mushroom Soup
1 jar	Chopped Pimento
1	Onion (finely chopped)
2	Green Bell Peppers (chopped)
	Lemon Juice
	Worcestershire Sauce
	Salt
	Pepper
	Accent

Mix in a large pot and heat ingredients thoroughly. Serve in chafing dish with Fritos. This recipe makes a large pot full, and can be cut down some.

WEST INDIES SALAD

½ c.   Salad Oil
½ c.   Water
½ c.   Apple Cider Vinegar
3 T.   Italian Dressing
1½ t. Creole Seasoning
3 T.   Lemon Juice
2 c.   Lump Crabmeat
1   med. Onion Chopped
       Salt and Pepper to taste

Mix ingredients, chill, and serve on crackers.

CATHARINE'S MINI BLT'S

Small Bread Rounds Toasted
Cherry Tomatoes
1 lb.   Bacon (Cooked and Crumbled)
2 T.   Mayonnaise
Dash of Yellow Mustard

Cut bread rounds with small biscuit cutter, and toast them. Mix bacon, mayonnaise, and mustard together. Cut cherry tomatoes in half, and top with bacon mixture. Place tomatoes on bread rounds.

This is a great little pick-up item that we have Catharine bring to anything from tailgating to a cocktail party. Catharine is like another sister to me and mine.

Neill Pitts, my sister, with Catharine Beasley O'Bryan

ELLEN'S CHEESE SPREAD

1 lb.	Grated Sharp Cheddar Cheese
2 c.	Hellmann's Mayonnaise
1 lb.	Cooked Crumbled Bacon
1 c.	Finely Chopped Onion
	Cayenne Pepper to taste

Mix ½ of ingredients in a blender, then add the remainder and mix. Hollow out a round loaf of French, or sourdough bread, and fill with the mixture. Serve on pieces of the bread, or crackers.

This makes quite a large portion, and can easily be halved. It keeps for a good while. Ellen is one of my sisters, and makes this for all of our parties.

BACON WRAPPED
WATER CHESTNUTS OR SHRIMP

2 cans	Whole Water Chestnuts
	or
½ lb.	Medium Shrimp – peeled and de-veined
½ lb.	Uncooked Bacon

MARINADE:

2 T.	Dark Brown Sugar
2 T.	Soy Sauce
2 T.	Worcestershire Sauce
4 T.	Lemon Juice
1 T.	Season Salt
2 cloves	Garlic (Substitute: 1T. Garlic Powder)

Marinate water chestnuts or shrimp in mixture at least 2 hours (overnight is fine too). Wrap 1/3 slice of uncooked bacon around the water chestnut or shrimp, and secure with a toothpick. Place on a broiler pan and bake at 375° for 15 to 20 minutes.

These are easy to reheat if necessary. You can also use chicken livers if you like.

MISS POLLY'S CRAB TOASTS

1 can	Crab Meat
	Lemon Juice
1 jar	Old English Cheese
1 stick	Butter
1 T.	Garlic Powder or Pressed Garlic
2 T.	Hellmann's Mayonnaise
	Cayenne Pepper
	Salt
1 pkg.	English Muffins

Drain Crab meat and sprinkle with lemon juice. Mix ingredients, and spread over halves of English muffins. Place on a cookie sheet and freeze. After they are thoroughly frozen, remove from the freezer, and cut into quarters. Put them in a storage bag, and return to the freezer. When ready to heat, place on a lightly greased cookie sheet, and bake at 350° for 15 minutes.

These can be made way ahead of time, and kept in the freezer until needed. They're great to have on hand in case of an emergency. I usually use a cooking spray on the cookie sheet.

Polly is my sister who lives in Florida. The neighbor children began to call her Miss Polly, and now her daughter, Katye does as well. The irony of all this is that people called our grandmother, for whom she is named Miss Polly. Many of the seafood recipes in the book are from Polly.

SALMON ON A BAGUETTE

SPREAD:

1 8 oz. pkg.	Cream Cheese (softened)
¼ c.	Chopped Red Onion
¼ c.	Capers (drained)
1 T.	Mayonnaise
	Tabasco sauce to taste

Mix ingredients adding the capers at the end.

SALMON:

1 pkg.	Smoked salmon
	Lemon Juice
	Dill weed

Cut salmon in bite size pieces. Sprinkle with lemon juice and dill weed. Refrigerate for a couple of hours. Cut baguette in small pieces, and spread with cream cheese mixture. Top with salmon, and serve.

The cream cheese spread will keep for a good while. You can also mix the spread and salmon together.

SHRIMP MOLD

3 lb.	Chopped Cooked Shrimp
3 lb.	Softened Cream Cheese
4 c.	Sour Cream
3 t.	Salt (maybe a little less)
12 t.	Lemon Juice
4 T.	Chopped Onion
6 T.	Chili Sauce
4 t.	Hot Sauce (Tabasco)
4 t.	A-1 Sauce
4 T.	Horseradish
4 t.	Worcestershire Sauce
4 t.	Diced Pimentos
4 t.	Chopped Parsley or Chives
1 can	Chicken Broth
3 T.	Gelatin

In a sauce pan, dissolve gelatin in chicken broth, and bring mixture to a boil. Let cool. Mix other ingredients, then add cooled broth. Pour into slightly greased fish molds and chill. Makes two molds. Serve on a tray with crackers. If you have trouble getting this out of the mold, run a knife around the edge of the mold.

Two of these molds go a long way. One is usually enough unless you're having a large party. This recipe is really easy to cut in half. It is a wonderful recipe, and we have had caterers ask us for it.

SHRIMP OR CRAB PUFFS

2 cans	Crescent Dinner Rolls
8 oz. pkg.	Cream Cheese
1 can	Shrimp or Crab
1 T.	Lemon Juice
1 T.	Sour Cream
½ c.	Shredded Parmesan Cheese (divided)
	Cayenne Pepper

Allow cream cheese to soften. Drain shrimp or crab, and add to cream cheese. Mix in lemon juice, sour cream, ¼ cup of Parmesan, and cayenne pepper. Press 2 triangles of crescent dough together, spread mixture, and roll up. Repeat until all of the dough is used. Refrigerate rolls for at least 30 minutes. Remove from refrigerator, and cut each roll into 5 pieces. Place on lightly greased cookie sheet, and top with Parmesan cheese. Bake at 375° for 12-15 minutes until golden brown. Yield 40.

The rolls can stay in the fridge for a while if necessary.

SAUSAGE PINWHEELS

1 lb.   **Sausage (hot or mild)**
1 can   **Crescent Rolls**

Spread crescent roll dough out, and pinch seams together. Spread sausage over the dough. Roll up, and wrap in aluminum foil. Freeze. Once thoroughly frozen, remove from freezer, and cut into pieces about ½ inch wide. Place on a cookie sheet, and bake at 350°-375° for about 15 to 20 minutes until brown.

These are especially good when having a breakfast, but can be used any time.

EMPANADAS

FILLING:

1 lb.	Lean Ground Beef or Ground Round
1	Medium Onion (finely chopped)
1-2	Small Cans of Green Chilies (chopped)
1 Clove	Garlic (pressed)
3 T.	Dry Onion Soup Mix
1 T.	Flour
1 4oz. Can	Black Olives – Chopped (optional)

Cook onion in a skillet with a small amount of oil until soft, but not browned. Add ground beef and brown. Drain. Add remaining ingredients, sprinkling flour over at the end. Add a little water if needed.

Pastry:
Prepared pastry dough. Roll pastry a little thinner than it comes, and cut with a large biscuit cutter.

Place a heaping tablespoon of filling on each pastry circle. Fold over, and press edges together with a fork. Prick top, and brush with milk. Place on a lightly greased cookie sheet, and bake at 375° for 12-15 minutes, or until lightly brown.
Serve with salsa and sour cream.

I got a variation of this recipe from a wonderful lady who used to bring these to the television tapings here in Nashville where I worked. Her name is Doris, but we all called her "the Goody Lady". Thanks to Doris for all the great treats

LAYERED NACHO DIP

1 16 oz. can	Refried Beans
½ pkg.	Taco Seasoning Mix
	Guacamole
1 c.	Sour Cream
1 4 ½ oz. can	Ripe Olives
2	Large Tomatoes (diced)
1 4 oz. can	Green Chilies
1 ½ c.	Monterey Jack Cheese

Combine beans and taco seasoning, and spread in a baking dish. Layer the rest of the ingredients in order. Bake until cheese melts. Serve with tortilla chips.

BAR-B-QUE SMOKIES

1 pkg.	Lil' Smokies
½ c.	Grape Jelly
1 T.	Mustard

In a sauce pan combine jelly and mustard. Add smokies. Serve in chafing dish with toothpicks.

SEASONED OYSTER CRACKERS

1 pkg.	Oyster Crackers
1 pkg.	Dry Ranch Dressing
½ c.	Vegetable or Corn Oil
2 t.	Dill Weed
¼ t.	Garlic Powder

Mix dressing, oil, dill weed, and garlic powder. Pour over oyster crackers in a food container or storage bag. Shake, and refrigerate until ready to serve.

These are great munchies to set around in bowls. In a cute container they make a good little gift.

BREAD STICKS

	Bread Cut in Strips or Triangles
3 T.	Melted Butter
½ t.	Lemon Pepper
¼ t.	Tabasco

Mix butter, lemon pepper, and Tabasco. Place bread on a cookie sheet. Brush both sides of bread with mixture. Bake 1-2 hours depending on the thickness of the bread at 200°. Allow to cool.

I often use the scraps from making bread rounds to make these. Be sure to cut the crust off.

DIP FOR VEGETABLES

2 c.	Sour Cream
4 oz.	Cream Cheese
3 T.	Tomato Paste
½ t.	Sugar
1 T.	Lemon Juice
3 T.	Chopped Parsley
1 t.	Basil
1	Clove Garlic (minced)
¼ t.	Black Pepper
¼ t.	Salt
3 T.	Chopped Onion

Combine ingredients, and serve with fresh raw vegetables.
This dip looks great in a hollowed out red cabbage.

Mozzarella Spread

Round Mozzarella Slices
Softened Cream Cheese
Pesto
Chopped Sun-dried Tomatoes
Toasted Pine Nuts

Line a square glass baking dish with plastic wrap. Place slices of mozzarella in the dish and spread with cream cheese. Then spread with pesto sauce, top with sun-dried tomatoes and toasted pine nuts. Fold plastic wrap over this and refrigerate. Remove and place on a plate with crackers when ready to serve.

NOTE: There are other items in later sections that make great hors d'oeuvres and appetizers.

Soups & Sandwiches

Soups & Sandwiches

TOMATO SANDWICHES

5-6	Small to Medium Tomatoes
4-5	Slices of Onion
	Parmesan Cheese
	Lemon Pepper
	Salt
	Black Pepper
	Vinegar
	Bread Rounds
1 c.	Hellmann's Mayonnaise
2 T.	Lemon Juice
	Cayenne Pepper to taste

Peel and slice tomatoes in fairly thin slices. You should be able to get 6-8 slices per tomato. Layer slices in a food container. Top with onion pieces. Sprinkle top layer with cheese, lemon pepper, salt and pepper, then splash vinegar over the top. Seal container and refrigerate at least 1 hour.

Cut bread rounds with biscuit cutters. Use two sizes that look to fit the tomatoes.

Mix mayonnaise, lemon juice and cayenne pepper. When ready to assemble, put tomatoes on a paper towel to get excess liquid off. Spread mayonnaise on bread rounds and top with a tomato. To fancy these up, add a small piece of parsley in the middle of the tomato. Serve on a tray.

NOTE: I always peel my tomatoes – it's a Southern thing. I highly recommend this. Also, Roma tomatoes don't work. In the winter, I find the best looking tomatoes I can, and ripen them a day or two. Be sure not to get large tomatoes.

These are always a hit. They go well at the fanciest cocktail party or the most casual tailgate.

Tomato Sandwiches

Hot/Cold Asparagus Roll-ups

Canned Asparagus Spears (drained)
Bread Triangles (crust removed)
Mayonnaise Mixture (see: Tomato Sandwiches)

Cut each piece of bread into two triangles. Spread with the mayonnaise. Place an asparagus spear at one end of the triangle and roll up. Serve this way, or once they are made, brush each with butter, place on a cookie sheet and toast in the oven.

This is another good party sandwich. I prefer them hot.

CUCUMBER SANDWICHES

Cucumber Slices
Vinegar
Water
Onion slices
Salt and pepper

Bread rounds

Mayonnaise Mixture (see: Tomato Sandwiches)

Score the cucumber with a fork and slice in fairly thin pieces. Put slices in a bowl and add slices of onion, vinegar, water, salt and pepper. Let set for a little while. Cut bread rounds with a biscuit cutter the size of the cucumber slices. Spread with mayonnaise, and top with slice of cucumber.

These look great on a tray with tomato sandwiches.

CREAM CHEESE, OLIVE, NUT SANDWICHES

2 -8oz. pkgs.	Cream Cheese (softened)
2 T.	Mayonnaise
½ c.	Green Olives (chopped)
½ c.	Chopped Pecans
	Tabasco

Mix well, and spread on sandwich bread. Makes 8-10 sandwiches.

For parties, cut the crust off the bread, and cut into bite size pieces. Men love these!

BECKY'S PIMENTO CHEESE SANDWICHES

8 oz.	American Cheese (grated)
8 oz.	Extra Sharp Cheddar Cheese (grated)
1 c.	Hellmann's Mayonnaise
1 - 4 oz. jar	Diced Pimentos
	Cayenne Pepper (to taste)

Grate cheese with a hand grater. A food processor grates too small. Mix in pimentos, mayonnaise, and pepper. Spread on sandwich bread.

This recipe came from my friend Becky. I just love it. For parties, cut the crust off of the bread, and then cut them into bite size triangles. To make it creamier, just add a little more mayonnaise.
Makes 8-10 sandwiches.

BETTY'S PIMENTO CHEESE

1 - 8 oz. block	Kraft Sharp Cheddar
1 - 8 oz. block	Kraft Extra Sharp Cheddar
1 - 2 med. jars	Pimentos
	Mayonnaise
	Salt

Betty says that the secret to good pimento cheese is grating the cheese the old-fashioned way – by hand. She uses mayonnaise to the extent that you don't have to add any more after it has been refrigerated when you are ready to spread it on sandwiches or crackers. Milder cheese may be used if you like.

Betty is my aunt.

My uncle and aunt, Jimmie and Betty Perkins.
Jimmie's recipe for Lamb Marinade is on page 179.

TOASTED MUSHROOM SANDWICHES

8 oz.	Fresh Mushrooms (chopped)
2 T.	Butter
1 T.	Worcestershire Sauce
2 T.	Onion (chopped)
2 T.	Sour Cream
	Tabasco
	Bread Rounds
	Melted Butter

Sauté onion in butter, Worcestershire, and Tabasco then add mushrooms, and sauté until cooked thoroughly. Add sour cream and remove from heat. Put a small amount of this mixture on a bread round, and top with another piece of bread. Brush both sides with butter. Place on a cookie sheet under the broiler. Toast both sides and serve.

CHEESE DREAMS

8 oz.	Extra Sharp Cheddar Cheese
1 T.	Onion (finely chopped)
1 T.	Mayonnaise
½ t.	Worcestershire Sauce
	Cayenne Pepper
	Bread
	Melted butter

In a processor, grate cheese, then remove from processor and add dough blade. Return cheese to processor bowl and add other ingredients. Mix until fairly smooth.
Spread on bread, and brush both sides of bread with butter. Place on cookie sheet, and place under broiler until each side is toasted. Cut in half, or even quarters before serving. Makes 4-6 sandwiches.

These are great with soups and salads. For parties, make them on bread rounds.

HAM & SWISS SANDWICHES

1 pkg.	Party Rolls or 6 Croissants
½ -3/4 lb.	Sliced Ham
1 - 8 oz. pkg.	Sliced Swiss Cheese

SPREAD:

1 stick	Butter
1-2 T.	Grated Onion
3 T.	Grey Poupon
2 T.	Worcestershire Sauce
1 ½ T.	Poppy Seeds

Mix all ingredients

Layer ham and Swiss cheese on bread spread top of the bread with mixture. Place on a baking pan and bake for about 30 minutes at 350°. Serve immediately.

These are great any time, and will hold up even long enough to take somewhere.

K.K. started making these, and now sister Neill (who does not cook much) fixes these as her staple for tailgating.

Mini Ruebens

Party Rye Bread
Corn Beef
Swiss Cheese
Sauerkraut
1000 Island Dressing
Butter

Make up sandwiches with all ingredients except butter. Butter each side of the bread and grill on a griddle or in a skillet.

Egg Salad Sandwiches

6	Hard Boiled Eggs
2 T.	Pickle Relish
1 ½ T.	Hellmann's Mayonnaise
½ T.	Yellow Mustard
½ t.	Durkees Sauce
¼ t.	Lemon Juice
¼ t.	Vinegar
	Salt and Pepper to taste

Chop eggs and add other ingredients. Spread on bread. Makes 6-8 sandwiches.
A really tasty alternative is to substitute chopped green olives (with pimentos) for the pickle relish.

BIG C'S GAZPACHO

1 lg. can	Tomato Juice
5	Ripe Tomatoes
	Chopped but not peeled
1 ½	Cucumbers
	Leave a little of the skin on and chop, but don't mush
3 T.	Chopped onion
1 jar	Diced Pimentos
1 lg. can	Chopped Mushrooms
4-5	Drops Garlic Juice
2-4 T.	Olive Oil
2 T.	Tarragon Vinegar
2 T.	Worcestershire
	Lots of Salt
	Pepper

Mix all ingredients and refrigerate. Serve with a dollop of sour cream.

Big C was Catharine's mother. This is the best gazpacho I've ever had.

CHICKEN ARTICHOKE SOUP

1/3 c.	Butter
3/4 c.	Flour
6 c.	Chicken Broth
1 c.	Warm Milk
1 c.	Warm Cream
1 ½-2 c.	Diced Chicken
2 cans	Chopped Artichoke Hearts
3 T.	Lemon Juice
½ t.	Salt
	Pepper to taste

Melt butter, add flour and cook until blended over low heat. Add 2 cups of chicken broth, warm milk and cream. Cook slowly stirring frequently until thick. Add remaining 4 cups of chicken broth, lemon juice, chicken and artichoke hearts. Then salt and pepper.

If you don't like artichokes, leave them and the lemon juice out, and have a cream of chicken soup. Or for something different add 1 tablespoon of tarragon and the lemon juice for a lemon chicken tarragon soup.

WHITE BEAN SOUP

2 lb.	White Beans (soak overnight in cold water)
1 lg.	Onion (chopped)
8 c.	Water
	Ham Bone
1 ½ c.	Chopped Ham
	Crushed Red Pepper
	Salt to taste

Combine beans, and onion in water with ham bone and some salt. Cook slowly until tender (about 3 hours). Add ham, red pepper and more salt. Cook for about one more hour. You may need to add some thickening (flour in a little water).
Serve with green onion and cornbread.

MAMA'S VEGETABLE SOUP

4 c.	Water
1	Medium Onion (chopped)
2 lb.	Stew Beef
1 lg. can	Whole Tomatoes
1 can	Tomato Sauce
2	Potatoes cut in 1" pieces (about 3c.)
4	Carrots cut in ½" pieces (about 2c.)
4 c.	Cabbage (cut up)
1 can	Cut Corn
1 can	Small Lima Beans
1 can	Cut Okra
1 T.	Worcestershire Sauce
2 t.	Vinegar
	Salt and Pepper to taste

In a large pot, place water, onion, and some salt and pepper. Cook until onion is tender. Add stew beef, and cook until it is tender. Then add potatoes, cabbage, and carrots, and cook until they start to become tender. Add tomatoes, sauce, and canned vegetables. Add seasonings and cook about 30 minutes. You may want to add some thickening (flour in a little water). It takes a good bit of salt, so taste and add until it's right for you.

This soup (and several others) is great with Hot Water Corn Cakes.
If you don't like these vegetables, choose your own.

We usually make the first pot of soup for Halloween. If there is any left, it's frozen and served Christmas Eve night.

GUMBO

3 med.	Onions – chopped
1	Green Bell Pepper – chopped
1 can	Tomato paste
4	Bay Leaves – crushed
2 t.	Dried Thyme
3 cloves	Garlic
1 lg. can	Peeled tomatoes
1 T.	Worcestershire Sauce
2 qt.	Water
2 lb.	Okra – cut in ¾ inch pieces
1 ½ lb.	Crabmeat
3 lb.	Shrimp – peeled
	Salt and Pepper to taste
	Tabasco
	Lemon juice
	Vinegar
ROUX:	
½ c.	Oil
1 c.	Flour

Cook roux until lightly brown. Add chopped onion and pepper and sauté until soft. Add tomato paste and cook until well blended, stirring as needed. Remove excess fat. Add salt, pepper, bay leaves, thyme, garlic, Tabasco, vinegar and lemon juice . Blend well. Add tomatoes and Worcestershire sauce and continue cooking. Add sliced okra that has been fried in oil and drained well. Add water a little at a time. When mixture begins to bubble, add crabmeat and uncooked shrimp. Cover and simmer slowly for about an hour. Taste and see if more seasoning is needed. Serve in soup bowls over cooked rice. Serves 16- 20.

CHILI

2 med.	Onions (chopped)
2 cloves	Garlic (minced)
1 lb.	Ground Beef
½ stick	Butter
1 T.	Chili Powder
1 lg. can	Tomato Sauce
1 sm. can	Tomato Paste
2 cans	Chili Beans in Sauce
1/8 t.	Crushed Red Pepper
	Salt and Pepper to taste
OPTIONS:	
	Spaghetti
	Tamales
	Jalapeno Peppers

Brown onions and garlic in butter. Add meat and brown. Season with salt and pepper. Add chili powder, tomato sauce, tomato pastes, 16 oz. of water, crushed red pepper, and some salt. Simmer 2 hrs. Add beans and heat thoroughly. Add any options. Serves 8-10.

Salads & Dressings

Salads & Dressings

CHICKEN SALAD

5 c.	Cooked Chicken (cut in small pieces)
1 c.	Chopped Celery
4	Chopped Hard-boiled Eggs
1 ¼ c.	Hellmann's Mayonnaise
1 ½ T.	Yellow Mustard
1 T.	Durkee's Sauce
2 T.	Lemon Juice
	Salt and Pepper to taste

Cook Chicken. Allow to cool and cut up. Combine all ingredients. Chill and serve in a tomato on lettuce, or on a sandwich. To use as an appetizer, spoon into a pastry shell and sprinkle with paprika.

I usually strain and keep some of the chicken broth to use in other dishes. It can be frozen.

LAYERED SALAD

3 c.	Shredded Lettuce
1 ½ c.	Chopped Green Pepper
2 c.	Chopped Celery
1 c.	Chopped Green Onions
1 can	Green Party Peas
1 can	Small Lima Beans
1 c.	Homemade Mayonnaise (on page 54)
4	Hardboiled Eggs (grated)
5	Strips of Bacon (cooked and crumbled)

In a deep bowl, layer all ingredients in order listed except bacon. Chill. Add bacon and serve. If you do not want to make mayonnaise, add some lemon juice and cayenne pepper to prepared mayonnaise.

HOMEMADE MAYONNAISE

2	Eggs (separated)
1 c.	Salad Oil
1 t.	Lemon Juice
1 t.	Vinegar
1/2 t.	Salt (slight)
1/8 t.	Paprika
1 T.	Mayonnaise
1 t.	Yellow Mustard

Separate eggs, and beat whites until they are stiff. Add yolks and continue to beat at high speed. Slowly add oil and continue beating at high to medium high. Scrape sides as needed once oil has been added which should take a while, add other ingredients and beat until thick. This could take 45 minutes or more. Once it is thick, pour into a jar and refrigerate.

FROZEN FRUIT SALAD

½ pint	Whipping Cream
1 T.	Mayonnaise
1 c.	Mini Marshmallows
1 can	Queen Ann Cherries (drained and cut in half)
1 can	Pineapple Tidbits (drained)
1 c.	Maraschino Cherries (cut in half)
1 c.	Chopped Pecans

Whip cream. Add mayonnaise and marshmallows. Mix well. Add fruit and pecans. Pour into and 8-inch square casserole dish and freeze. Cut in squares and serve on a piece of lettuce with a dollop of mayonnaise.

This is easy to double.

CONGEALED CRANBERRY SALAD

1 Lg. or 2 Sm. pkg.	Black Cherry Jell-O
1 c.	Boiling Water
½ c.	Sugar
1 T.	Lemon Juice
1 tub	Ocean Spray Cran-Orange
1 c.	Crushed Pineapple (drained)
½ c.	Chopped Pecans

Dissolve Jell-O and sugar in water. Add lemon juice, then other ingredients. Mix well, and pour into 8-inch square casserole. Chill until hardened. Cut in squares and serve on a piece of lettuce. Top with a dollop of mayonnaise.

We always have Cranberry Salad on Holidays.

Mrs. Brown's Frozen Fruit Salad

2 – 15oz. cans	Mixed fruit (not Fruit Cocktail)
½ lb.	Marshmallows
1 c.	Toasted Almonds
1 pt.	Whipped Cream

DRESSING:

4	Egg Yolks
4 T.	Vinegar
4 T.	Sugar

Cook dressing in double boiler until thick. Add marshmallows and cook until mixed and melted. Cool. Add fruit and almonds to dressing. Fold in whipped cream, and mix well. Freeze in a 3 qt. oblong casserole. Cut in pieces to serve. Serves 12 – 15.

JEAN CRAWFORD'S VEGETABLE SALAD

2 – 16 oz. cans	LeSueur Party Green Peas
2 – 16 oz. cans	White or Yellow Corn
2 – 16 oz. cans	French Style Green Beans
2 – 15 oz. cans	Artichoke Hearts (chopped)
1 c.	Chopped Purple Onion
2 c.	Chopped Celery
2 c.	Chopped Green Bell Pepper

Drain all cans and mix in a large bowl. Makes 1 gallon.

DRESSING:

1½ c.	Sugar
1 c.	Salad Oil
1 c.	Apple Cider Vinegar
1 t.	Salt
1 t.	Pepper

Combine dressing ingredients and mix in mixer or food processor.
Pour over vegetables, and refrigerate.

This is a recipe of a friend of my mother's. It will keep for weeks in the fridge. Since it makes so much, you may want to half it, which is easy to do.

PASTA SALAD

1 pkg.	Spiral Shaped Tri-Colored Pasta
½ c. each	Green, Red, and Yellow Bell Pepper (chopped)
¾ c.	Ripe Olives (chopped)
¼ c.	Grated Parmesan Cheese
1 t.	Garlic Powder
1 c.	Creamy Caesar Salad Dressing

OPTIONAL ITEMS:

1 c.	Green Peas
or	
2 c.	Chicken (grilled or just cooked and cut in strips)

Cook and drain pasta. Add all ingredients except dressing, and mix well. Add dressing and toss. Refrigerate and serve.

The pasta really absorbs the Caesar dressing, so you might need to add more after it has been refrigerated. This can be doubled or tripled for a large group.

This is another of K.K.'s concoctions.

RICE SALAD

1 pkg.	Lipton's Roasted Chicken Flavored Rice
1 can	Artichoke Hearts (chopped)
¾ c.	Chopped Green Olives
½ c.	Chopped Green Onions
1 c.	Mayonnaise

Mix all ingredients and refrigerate.

I think that this came from our cousin, Judy Harris.

SLAW

16 oz.	Cabbage – shredded or Slaw Mix
	Carrots – shredded – if not using Slaw

MIX

1 c.	Mayonnaise
1½ T.	Vinegar
1 t.	Sugar
1 t.	Season Salt
½ t.	Salt
¼ t.	Pepper

Mix ingredients and chill before serving. Serves 10 – 12.

We always have Neill make this, and serve it with many of our meals. Mama says you have to have slaw with green beans.

POTATO SALAD

6 medium	Potatoes (cubed)
1 c.	Celery (chopped)
4	Hard boiled Eggs (chopped)
½ c.	Onion (chopped)
½ c.	Sweet Pickle Relish
1 T.	Lemon Juice
1½ t.	Salt
½ t.	Black Pepper
1 c.	Mayonnaise
2-3 T.	Mustard
2 T.	Durkee's Sauce
	Paprika

Cook potatoes in their skins about 1 hour until they are done. Poke with a fork to see if they are cooked thoroughly. Do not over cook, or the potatoes will fall apart and be mushy. Peel potatoes and cut into cubes while they are still warm. The cooler they get, the stickier they become. Add other ingredients and mix well. Refrigerate at least until chilled. This can be kept overnight. It takes a while for the flavors to mix. After bringing it out of the refrigerator, taste to see if it needs any more seasoning.

Sprinkle with paprika before serving. Serves 10-12.

CORNBREAD SALAD

1 recipe	Cornbread – Cooked
½ c.	Sweet Pickle Relish
4 large	Ripe Tomatoes (diced)
½ c.	Celery (finely chopped)
1 c.	Green Bell Pepper (finely chopped)
1 c.	Chopped Onion
1 lb.	Bacon (cooked and crumbled)
1 can	Sliced Water Chestnuts

Break cornbread into good size pieces (not small crumbs).
Mix all ingredients, and place in 9" X 12" pan.

DRESSING:

1 c.	Mayonnaise
1/4 c.	Sweet Pickle Juice
1/2 t.	Sugar
	Cayenne pepper to taste

Mix dressing and pour over salad. Refrigerate a few hours and serve.

WILTED LETTUCE SALAD

3 – 4 c.	Green or Red Leaf Lettuce – broken up
3 T.	Red Onion – chopped
4 slices	Bacon
2 T.	Vinegar
	Salt and Pepper to taste

TOP WITH:

Cherry or Grape Tomatoes
Tortilla Strips
Fresh Mushrooms – sliced

Fry bacon and remove from skillet. Mix lettuce and onion in a serving bowl. In the skillet used to cook the bacon add vinegar, salt and pepper to the bacon grease and heat thoroughly. Add crumbled bacon to this mixture. When well heated, pour mixture over lettuce mixture and top with tomatoes, mushrooms and tortilla strips. Serves 6-8.
If you want to add cheese, I'd suggest goat cheese or something soft like that.

RAMEN NOODLE SLAW

1 head	Cabbage (shredded)
1	Red Bell Pepper (chopped)
4-5	Green Onions
1 pkg.	Chicken Ramen Noodles
1/3 c.	Sesame Seeds
½ c.	Slivered Almonds
3 T.	Margarine or Butter

DRESSING:

½ c.	Salad Oil
½ c.	Red Wine Vinegar
½ c.	Water
½ c.	Sugar
½ t.	Salt
¼ t.	Garlic Powder
¼ t.	Pepper

Mix cabbage, bell pepper and green onions. Sauté sesame seeds, almonds and seasoning package from noodles in melted butter until toasted. Mix dressing. Right before serving toss dressing, almonds, sesame seeds and broken up noodles in the cabbage. Serves 10-12.

TOMATO ASPIC

2 pts.	Tomato Juice
2 T.	Lemon Juice
1 t.	Sugar
½	Bay Leaf (remove after cooking)
2 T.	Gelatin in ½ c. water
2 stalks	Celery – chopped
1 small	Onion –grated
½ c.	Green Olives – sliced
½ c.	Artichoke Hearts – chopped
1 T.	Worcestershire Sauce
	Salt & Pepper to taste

Combine first 4 ingredients and cook over low heat 10 to 15 minutes. Remove from heat and pour in gelatin mixture. Stir until dissolved. Add the rest of the ingredients. Pour into molds or greased pyrex and refrigerate until firm.

FAUCON SALAD DRESSING

2	Lemons – juiced
2	Eggs – lightly beaten
2 c.	Salad Oil
2 T.	Vinegar from Pickled Onions
1 t.	Tabasco
1 T.	Worcestershire Sauce
1 t.	Salt
1 clove	Garlic
4	Hard Boiled Eggs – finely chopped
12	Pickled Cocktail Onions – finely chopped
½ lb.	Roquefort Cheese – crumbled
2 T.	Hellmann's Mayonnaise

Place eggs and lemon juice in mixing bowl or processor. Beat at high speed and add oil slowly. Mix until thick, then other ingredients except chopped egg, onions, garlic, cheese and mayonnaise. Mix well, then fold in the rest of the ingredients. Leave garlic clove in mixture one or two days, then remove. Serve over lettuce wedges and top with crumbled bacon.

NOTE: This recipe contains uncooked eggs.

SPINACH SALAD & DRESSING

SALAD:

Spinach
Grated Hardboiled Eggs
Chopped Purple Onion
Sliced Fresh Mushrooms
Mandarin Oranges
Cooked and Crumbled Bacon
Sliced Almonds

We usually put each ingredient in its own bowl, and let people put what they want in their salad.

DRESSING:

3 T.	Finely Grated Onion
1 t.	Worcestershire Sauce
1/3 c.	Catsup
¼ c.	Apple Cider Vinegar
2/3 c.	Sugar
¼ t.	Salt
	Cayenne Pepper to taste
1 c.	Salad Oil

Combine all ingredients except oil in food processor. Mix until well blended, then slowly add oil. Refrigerate. This is better if it is made a day ahead of time.

FRESH FRUIT SALAD
WITH POPPY SEED DRESSING

SALAD:

2c. each cut up:

Cantaloupe

Honey Dew Melon

Watermelon

Pineapple

Grapes (seedless red or green)

Strawberries

Or any other fresh fruit you like

DRESSING:

½ c.	Sugar
1/3 c.	Honey
1 t.	Onion Juice
6 T.	Tarragon Vinegar
3 T.	Lemon Juice
1 c.	Salad Oil
1 t.	Dry Mustard
1 t.	Paprika
¼ t.	Salt
2 t.	Poppy seeds

Soak poppy seeds in water 2 hours. Mix dry ingredients. Add other ingredients except oil and poppy seeds. Place in mixer or food processor. Add oil slowly while mixing. Add poppy seeds last. Should be very thick. Dressing will keep for weeks in the refrigerator.

We usually serve the dressing on the side, and also slice some bananas on the side.

SESAME SEED DRESSING

1 c.	Sugar
1 t.	Paprika
½ t.	Ground Mustard
1 t.	Salt
1 t.	Worcestershire Sauce
1 T.	Fresh Onion Juice
1 c.	Apple Cider Vinegar
2 c.	Salad Oil
1 jar	Toasted Sesame Seeds

Toast sesame seeds on a cookie sheet in a 300° oven about 20 minutes. Don't let them get dark. Mix sugar, paprika, mustard, salt, Worcestershire, and onion juice in a mixer or food processor until well blended. Gradually add oil, beating constantly, and then do the same with the vinegar. Add sesame seeds at the end.

This will keep indefinitely in the refrigerator. Shake well before using. It is great on most salads, and fruit as well.

Sesame Seed Dressing

BOBBY'S QUICK & EASY DRESSING FOR FRUIT

¼ c. **Honey**
1 **Lime (juiced)**
1 t. **Mint (chopped)**
Dash of Cinnamon

Mix ingredients and pour over cut up fruit.

Our friend Bobby's name for the recipe is longer than the ingredient list, but this is really a quick and easy way to add zest to a bowl of you favorite fruits.

HONEY MUSTARD DRESSING

1 c.	Mayonnaise
¼ c.	Honey
¼ c.	Prepared Mustard
1 t.	Horseradish
	Cayenne Pepper

Combine ingredients in mixing bowl or processor. Mix on low speed until smooth. Chill and serve over salads.

BLEU CHEESE DRESSING

1 qt.	Mayonnaise
1	Lemon – juiced
1 c.	Salad Oil
1/3 c.	Vinegar
¼ t.	Sugar
¼ t.	Salt
¼ clove	Garlic – Chopped or 1/8 t. Garlic Powder
1 lb.	Bleu Cheese – Crumbled

Mix all ingredients except cheese in a mixing bowl or processor at medium speed until thoroughly blended. Add bleu cheese on low speed. Chill and serve over salads.

FRENCH DRESSING

1 c.	Sugar
¾ c.	Tarragon Vinegar
1 c.	Salad Oil
1½ t.	Paprika
1 t.	Salt
2 buds	Garlic – Finely Chopped

Mix ingredients in a jar. Refrigerate 24 hours. Sake well before using

Eggs, Rice & Pasta

Eggs, Rice & Pasta

SAUSAGE EGG CASSEROLE

1 lb.	Mild Sausage (cooked & crumbled)
9	Eggs
1½ c.	Grated Sharp Cheddar Cheese
3 c.	Milk
1½ t.	Dry Mustard
1 t.	Salt
3 slices	White Bread Cut in ¼" Cubes

Place bread in the bottom on a 3 quart casserole. In a bowl, beat eggs. Combine other ingredients in the bowl with the eggs. Pour mixture over bread. Bake in a 350° oven for 1 hour, or until set.

EGGS VERMICELLI CASSEROLE

2 c.	White Sauce
¾ c.	Parmesan Cheese
1½ t.	Worcestershire Sauce
1 c.	Bread Crumbs
6	Hard Boiled Eggs (grated)
6	Slices of Bacon (cooked and crumbled)

Make white sauce (see page 174), add Worcestershire sauce and ½ c. Parmesan cheese. In a casserole dish (1 ½ qt.), layer 1/3 of the bread crumbs, ½ of the eggs, ½ of the bacon, and ½ of the cream sauce. Repeat. Top with remaining bread crumbs and ¼ c. Parmesan cheese. Dot with butter. Bake at 400° about 20 –25 min. until brown. Serves 6-8.

BASIC QUICHE

1	Deep Dish Pastry Shell (partially cooked)
4	Eggs (beaten)
1 c.	Whipping Cream
1 c.	Grated Swiss Cheese
1 t.	Salt
	Cayenne Pepper to Taste

Cook pastry shell at 400° for 8-10 minutes. Mix ingredients together, and pour over variation mixture. Bake at 375° for about 35 minutes. Let stand for 5 minutes before serving. Serves 6-8.

See following pages for a variety of quiche fillers.

LORRAINE QUICHE

6-7 pieces	Bacon (cooked and crumbled)
2 T.	Grated Onion
2 T.	Dijon Mustard
2 t.	Chopped Italian Parsley

Mix bacon, onion, and mustard, then spread in the bottom of the pastry shell. Pour Basic Quiche egg mixture over this. Sprinkle parsley over the top after quiche is cooked. Note: Because of the bacon in this recipe, you might want to cut the salt in half.

SPINACH QUICHE

1 c.	Chopped Frozen Spinach
2 T.	Butter
1 T.	Lemon Juice
1 clove	Garlic Minced

Thaw and drain spinach. Sauté garlic in melted butter about 1 minute. Add spinach and lemon juice and sauté another 3-5 minutes until liquid is cooked off. Spread in the bottom of the pastry shell, cover with the Basic Quiche egg mixture, and bake.

CHICKEN & BROCCOLI QUICHE

¾ c.	Broccoli Florets
¾ c.	Cooked Chicken (cubed)
4 T.	Chicken Broth
1 T.	Butter
1 T.	Lemon Juice

Melt butter in a skillet, add broth, lemon juice and broccoli. Cover and cook about 5 minutes, and add chicken. Cook until liquid has evaporated. Put in the bottom of the pastry shells, cover with the Basic Quiche egg mixture and bake.

MUSHROOM QUICHE

1 c.	Sliced Mushrooms
3 T.	Butter
2 T.	Grated Onion
1 clove	Garlic (minced)

Sauté onion and garlic in melted butter about 2 minutes. Add mushrooms and sauté until tender. Place in the bottom of the pastry shell, add Basic Quiche egg mixture and bake.

SHRIMP & CRAB QUICHE

1 can	Baby Shrimp
1 can	Crab Meat
2 T.	Lemon Juice

Drain both shrimp and crab. Mix together with lemon juice. Spread in the bottom of the pastry shell, add Basic Quiche egg mixture and bake.

OMELET

2 T.	Butter or cooking oil
3	Eggs – lightly beaten
1 T.	Milk or cottage cheese
	Salt and Pepper
½ c.	Shredded Cheese

Melt butter in skillet. Beat eggs with milk, add salt and pepper. Pour in skillet. When almost done, add cheese and flip into omelet. If cooking an omelet with onion, peppers, mushrooms, or raw vegetables, sauté the ingredients in the butter first, and then add the egg mixture. Use your imagination when selecting ingredients and cheeses.

BRIE SAUSAGE EGG CASSEROLE

10 oz.	Brie
1 lb.	Hot Sausage
6 pieces	White Bread
1 c.	Grated Parmesan
8	Eggs
3 c.	Whipping Cream
2 c.	Fat Free Milk
1 t.	Season Salt
1 t.	Dry Mustard

Discard rind from Brie, and cut in cubes. Cook and drain sausage. Cut crust from bread. Place crust in bottom of a 3-quart baking dish, and bread on top. Put crumbled sausage on top of bread, then Brie and Parmesan. In a bowl beat 6 eggs, add 2 cups of whipping cream, fat free milk, season salt, and mustard. Mix well and pour over cheese. Cover and chill 8 hours. Then add mixture of 2 eggs beaten and 1 cup whipping cream. Sprinkle top with Parmesan and chopped green onions. Bake at 350 degrees for 1 hour, or until set.

CHEESE SOUFFLÉ

10 slices	White Bread (crust removed)
3 T.	Softened Butter
8 oz.	Extra Sharp Cheddar Cheese
4	Eggs
2 c.	Milk
1 t.	Salt
1 t.	Worcestershire Sauce
½ t.	Dry Mustard
	Cayenne Pepper

Butter bread, and put ½ of the bread, cheese, eggs, and milk into a blender or processor. Blend at high speed until thoroughly mixed. Add remainder of the ingredients, and blend thoroughly. Pour into a greased 1½ qt. casserole, and bake at 350° for 1 hour. Serves 6-8. This can be mixed ahead of time. It is easy to double

CHEESE GRITS

2 c.	Grits
8 c.	Water
1 T.	Salt
1	Egg (beaten)
2 c.	Sharp Cheddar Cheese (grated)
1 t.	Black Pepper
1 T.	Worcestershire Sauce
1 t.	Garlic Powder or 2 cloves of garlic minced
1 stick	Butter
	Cayenne Pepper to taste

In a pot (at least 3qt.), bring water with salt added to a boil. Add grits, lower heat, and cook about 8-10 minutes. Add butter and 1½ c. cheese, Worcestershire sauce, pepper, and garlic. Mix until cheese and butter melt. Add beaten egg. Pour into greased baking dish. Top with remaining ½c. of cheese. Bake in a 350˚ oven for 45 minutes to 1 hour. Serves 16-18.

WILD JUDY'S RICE

8 oz.	Wild Rice
¼ - ½ c.	Orzo
4-5 c.	Chicken Stock
2 T.	Butter
2 T.	Olive Oil
¼ c.	White Wine
1 box	Fresh Mushrooms (sliced)
½ c.	Red or White Onion (chopped)
2 cloves	Garlic (finely chopped)
1	Red Bell Pepper (diced)
¼ c.	Red Onion (chopped)
3-4	Green Onions (sliced)
1 can	Whole Yellow Kernel Corn (8¾ oz.)
1 can	Water Chestnuts (coarsely chopped)
	Flat Leaf Italian Parsley

ADD TO TASTE:

Salt and Pepper

Soy Sauce

Olive Oil

Dried Cranberries (chopped)

Sliced or Slivered Almonds

Susan with Judy Traughber

Cook wild rice at a slow boil covered approximately 45 minutes in 4 cups of chicken broth until some kernels start to pop open on the ends. Drain in colander and cool.

Cook orzo approximately 6 minutes in salted water until al dente. Drain in colander and cool. Sauté in butter, olive oil and white mushrooms, onion, and garlic until almost all of the juice has evaporated, then cool in the same pan. Mix all ingredients together. Be sure to add the juices from the sauté mixture. Refrigerate. Serve at room temperature or microwave to heat. To use as a main dish add grilled chicken.

My high school friend makes this, and I just love it.

BETTY B'S FETTUCCINE

1 lb.	Fettuccine
1 stick	Butter
2 c.	Grated Swiss Cheese
1 c.	Grated Parmesan Cheese
1 pt.	Half and Half
1 small can	Mushroom pieces (use large can if you like)
	Cayenne Pepper to taste

Cook and drain noodles. Melt butter in pot. Mix in noodles and other ingredients. Pour into greased casserole dish, and bake at 350° until bubbly. About 30 minutes. Serves 10-12. This will freeze. This is a wonderful side dish that is great with grilled chicken or shrimp.

RICE CASSEROLE

1 stick	Butter
1 c.	Long Grain Rice
1 can	French Onion Soup
1 can	Sliced Water Chestnuts - Undrained
4 oz. can	Sliced Mushrooms - Drained

Melt butter in 2-quart casserole. Mix other ingredients. Cover with foil and bake at 350° for 45 minutes. Uncover and bake for 15 more minutes.

This is another item that K.K. usually makes for family gathering, always at Easter.

RISOTTO WITH PARMESAN

5 c.	Chicken Broth (canned is OK)
6 T.	Butter
1 ½ c.	Finely Chopped Onion
1 ½ c.	Arborio Rice (Italian short grain rice)
1 ½ c.	Grated Parmesan
3 T.	Fresh Italian Parsley (chopped)
	Cayenne Pepper
	Salt
	Shaved Parmesan

Bring broth to a boil in a medium sauce pan, then reduce heat to low and cover. Melt 3 T. butter in a heavy medium saucepan on medium-low heat. Add onion and sauté until tender, but not brown. (about 10-15 min.) Increase heat to medium and add rice. Stir 1 minute. Add 1½ c. warm broth. Boil gently until broth is absorbed, stirring frequently. Add 1c. of broth and stir until it is absorbed. Add remaining 2½ c. of broth ½ c. at a time allowing broth to be absorbed before adding more. Stir frequently until rice is tender, and mixture is creamy. About 25 minutes. Stir in 3 T. butter and 1½ c. Parmesan cheese. Add salt and cayenne pepper to taste. Pour mixture in a serving bowl and top with parsley and shaved Parmesan.

LASAGNA

1 box	Lasagna Noodles
16 oz.	Ricotta Cheese
½ c.	Parmesan Cheese
2	Eggs (beaten)
2 T.	Parsley (chopped)
2-8 oz. pkgs.	Mozzarella Cheese Slices
3-4 c.	Meat Sauce (see recipe)

Cook lasagna noodles in salt water. Mix ricotta, Parmesan, eggs, and parsley. In a large casserole dish (3qt.) Layer noodles, meat sauce, mozzarella, and ricotta mixture. Repeat until casserole is almost full. Top with more mozzarella and parmesan. Bake at 350° for 45 minutes to 1 hour until bubbly. Serves 12 – 15.

This freezes well, and can also be made up a day ahead to time.

Vegetables

Vegetables

GREEN BEAN CASSEROLE

2 boxes	Frozen French Style Green Beans
1 can	Cream of Mushroom Soup
½ stick	Butter
1 can	Sliced Water Chestnuts
1 can	French Fried Onion Rings
	Salt and Pepper

Cook beans as directed. Drain. Melt butter in casserole dish. In a separate bowl mix beans, soup, water chestnuts, salt and pepper to taste. Pour mixture into baking dish and cook at 350° for 20-30 minutes. Add onion rings to top, and cook until brown (about 5 minutes).

GREEN BEANS

1 ½ to 2 lbs.	Fresh Green Beans
or	
2 lg. cans	Green Beans
1 med.	Onion
2 T.	Vinegar
1 t.	Sugar
1 T.	Salt
1 t.	Pepper

Clean beans and break in two or three pieces each depending on the size of the beans. Place in a large pot and cover with water. Add other ingredients and cook at a slow boil until tender – usually 2-3 hours. Taste and add more salt or pepper if needed. Spoon out with a slotted spoon into a bowl and serve. I use pole beans. They are really the best. Serve with green onions.

ASPARAGUS

1-2 lbs.	Fresh Asparagus
1 T.	Lemon Juice
2 T.	Butter
	Salt, Pepper, and Lemon Pepper

Put a small amount of water in a sauce pan that will hold the number of asparagus spears you are cooking. Add lemon juice, butter, salt, pepper, and lemon pepper. Bring to a boil. Add asparagus that have been cleaned, and have had the ends removed, and cover. Reduce heat and cook for 4-5 minutes. Uncover and check to see if they are done enough. They should be crisp. Don't allow them to cook too long, or they will be too limp. Remove from water, and serve with Hollandaise Sauce (see page 172).

ASPARAGUS CASSEROLE

3 cans	Asparagus Spears
3	Hard Boiled Eggs (sliced)
1 can	Cream of Mushroom Soup
1 c.	Sour Cream
1 c.	Sharp Cheddar Cheese
1 T.	Lemon Juice

Drain asparagus and place in a casserole dish. Cover with sliced eggs. In a bowl, mix other ingredients, withholding ¼ c. of the cheese. Cover eggs with mixture, and then sprinkle the top with remainder of cheese. Bake for 20-30 minutes at 350°.

You might want to use more cheese. This is a great holiday dish.

CORN PUDDING

5	Eggs (beaten)
¾ c.	Sugar
3 c.	Frozen Shoe Peg Corn
2 c.	Milk
3 T.	Melted Butter
1 t.	Salt
	White Pepper to taste

Melt butter in 1½ - 2 qt. casserole dish and allow to cool. Mix other ingredients and add to dish. Cook 30 – 45 minutes until firm at 350°. Serves 8.

This is too yummy!

FRIED CORN

6 ears	**Fresh White Corn** (Silver Queen or Truckers)
4-5 pieces	**Bacon**
½ T.	**Flour**
2 T.	**Butter**
	Salt and Pepper to taste

Shuck corn and cut off the cob. Do not scrape the cob too much, because you don't want to have pieces of the cob in the corn. Cover with water. In a skillet cook bacon and remove to cool. Keep the bacon grease in the skillet. Pour corn and water in skillet and cook, stirring often. Add salt and pepper. Cook until tender. Do not let it get dry. Add more water as it cooks down. It will probably need to cook about an hour. When almost done, sprinkle in the flour. Add butter at the end. It should not be watery when it's ready. Pour into a bowl and top with crumbled bacon. Serves 8 –10.

SQUASH CASSEROLE

2 lb.	Yellow Squash
1 sm.	Onion (cut in several pieces)
1/3 c.	Milk
½ stick	Butter
1 c.	Egg
¾ t.	Salt
¼ t.	Pepper
1 can	French Fried Onion Rings
	Salt and Pepper to taste

Clean squash and cut into pieces about ¾ inch long. Place squash, onion, salt and pepper in a pot and cover with water. Bring to a boil. Reduce heat and cover. Cook about 20 minutes until tender. Drain in a colander, and then pour into a baking dish (1½ to 2 qt.). Mix in butter, milk and egg. Salt and pepper to taste. Bake at 350° for about 30 minutes until firm (but don't dry it out). Top with onion rings and cook about 5 minutes until brown. Serves 10 – 12.

Option:
½ c.   Grated Sharp Cheddar Cheese

This should be added when mixing in the other ingredients.

Squash Casserole

Fresh Limas, Crowder or Black Eyed Peas, Etc.

1 ½ - 2 lbs.   **Fresh Beans or Peas (cleaned and sorted)**
4-5 T.   **Butter**
Salt and Pepper

Place beans or peas in a pot and cover with water. Add salt and pepper along with 2T. of butter. Bring to a boil, then reduce heat and cook until tender. Salt and pepper to taste. Spoon into a bowl with a slotted spoon and add 2-3T. of butter.

This is really the way to do any of these wonderful fresh beans or peas. You can use frozen if you can't get fresh. Serves 8-10.

MASHED POTATOES

6-8 lg.	White Potatoes
6 T.	Butter
¾ c.	Sour Cream
¼ c.	Milk
1/3 c.	Grated Sharp Cheddar Cheese
	Salt and Pepper

Peel potatoes and cut into pieces about ¾ to 1 inch. Place in a pot and cover with water. Add salt and pepper. Bring to a boil, then reduce heat and cover. Cook about 20-25 minutes until tender. Drain and immediately place in mixing bowl. Add butter, sour cream, and milk and beat until fluffy and creamy. Salt and pepper to taste. Add more sour cream or milk if needed. Pour into baking dish, top with cheese and bake at 350° until hot and cheese has melted (about 15 minutes). Serves 10-12.

TWICE BAKED POTATOES

4 lg.	Baking Potatoes
4 T.	Butter
½ c.	Sour Cream
¼ c.	Milk
¾ c.	Sharp Cheddar Cheese (grated)
	Salt and Pepper

Clean potatoes and bake in 350° oven about 1 hour. Remove from oven and cut in half length wise. Remove potato from skin with a spoon and place in a mixing bowl.

Add other ingredients except ¼ c. of cheese and beat until creamy. Spoon mixture back into potato skins and top with cheese. Return to 350° oven and cook until hot and cheese has melted. The potatoes must be beaten while they are still hot, or they will become lumpy. Serves 8. Option: Top with cooked and crumbled bacon. These can be frozen, so fix more than you need, and throw the rest in the freezer.

POTATO CASSEROLE

1- 2 lb. bag	Hash Brown Potatoes
2 cans	Cream of Mushroom Soup
1 stick	Butter
3 T.	Grated Onion
2 c.	Grated Sharp Cheddar Cheese
2 c.	**Sour Cream**

Melt butter in a 3qt. casserole dish. Mix the rest of the ingredients in a large bowl, except ½ c. of cheese. Allow casserole to cool, then pour potato mixture into the dish. Top with the rest of the cheese, and bake at 325° for 1½ hours. Serves 15-18.

This can be halved for a smaller group, or put it in 2 smaller casseroles, and freeze one. Even though you're using frozen potatoes, after they are cooked, they can be refrozen.

MASHED SWEET POTATOES

6-8	Sweet Potatoes
1 stick	Butter
¾ c.	White Sugar
¾ c.	Dark Brown Sugar
¼ t.	Lemon Juice

TOPPING:

Marshmallows

Peel potatoes and cut into 1 inch pieces. Place in a pot with water and cook until tender. Drain and pour into mixing bowl. Add other ingredients except marshmallows and whip until creamy. Pour into a casserole (2-3 qt.). Cook at 350° about 15-20 minutes. Remove from the oven and top with marshmallows. Return to the oven for about 5 minutes until marshmallows are lightly browned. Keep a close watch on the marshmallows, because they will burn before you know it. Serves 10-12.

CANDIED SWEET POTATOES

6-8	Sweet Potatoes
1 stick	Butter
¾ c.	White Sugar
1 c.	Dark Brown Sugar
¼ t.	Lemon Juice
	Water

Peel potatoes and cut in thin pieces, about ¼ to ½ inch slices. Place in a 3 qt. casserole and add water. Add other ingredients and cook at 350° about 45 minutes to 1 hour until potatoes are tender. Stir occasionally and add more water if needed. Don't add too much water. You want the sugar and butter to make a fairly thick syrup.

These cook down quite a bit. When you start, you want the casserole to be really full. Serves 10-12.

BAKED APPLES

10-12	Cooking Apples
1 c.	Sugar
1 stick	Butter
¼ t.	Lemon Juice
	Water

Core and slice cleaned apples into thin pieces. Place in a 3 qt. casserole dish and cover with water. Add other ingredients. Bake at 350° for about 45 minutes to 1 hour until tender. Stir occasionally and add more sugar if necessary. Don't allow to stick or get too dried out. You may need to add a little more water. Just like the candied sweet potatoes, these cook down quite a bit. Serves 10-12

BAKED TOMATOES

8-10 med.	Tomatoes
1 pkg.	Frozen Spinach Soufflé
4 T.	Parmesan Cheese
½ t.	Salt
¼ t.	Pepper

Thaw spinach soufflé. Cut out the tops of the tomatoes and core out the center. Place tomatoes on baking dish. Mix salt and pepper into spinach and spoon into tomatoes. Top with Parmesan cheese. Bake at 350° for 30 – 45 minutes. Serves 8-10.

VEGETABLE CASSEROLE

1 pkg. each   Frozen Baby Limas
Frozen French Style Green Beans
Frozen Baby Green Peas

Cook together in salted water, and drain in a colander.

SAUCE:
1 c.	Mayonnaise
4	Hard-boiled Eggs (chopped)
3 T.	Onion (chopped)
1 T.	Worcestershire sauce
1½ T.	Lemon juice
	Cayenne pepper

TOPPING:
1 can	French Fried Onion Rings

Mix ingredients and heat.
Pour vegetables into a casserole dish (1½ - 2 qt.), and then pour heated mixture over them. Heat in 325° oven about 15 minutes, then top with onion rings and heat another 5 minutes or so until brown. Serves 6-8.

This can also be served cold. When serving cold, refrigerate after pouring on mixture, and don't use the onion rings.

EGGPLANT CASSEROLE

1 med.	Eggplant
2 slices	Bacon (diced and fried)
1 med.	Onion (chopped)
1 med.	Potato (grated)
1 can	Cream of Chicken & Mushroom Soup
1 t.	Worcestershire Sauce
½ c.	Crumbled Ritz Crackers
2 T.	Butter
	Salt
	Cayenne Pepper

Cut eggplant into 1" slices, and soak in salted water for 10 minutes. Cook in salted water another 10 minutes and drain. Fry diced bacon in a large skillet until crisp, and remove from skillet. Leave the grease in the skillet and stir in onion and potato. Cook for about 10 minutes until potato is done, stirring occasionally. In a large bowl mix eggplant, onion-potato mixture, bacon, soup, and cayenne pepper. Salt if necessary. Pour into 1½ qt. greased baking dish. Sprinkle top with melted butter and cracker crumbs. Bake at 350° for 30-35 minutes. Serves 6-8.

TURNIP GREENS

2-3 lbs.	Fresh Turnip Greens
1 med.	Onion
1- 4 oz. piece	Hog Jowl or Country Bacon
1 t. +	Salt
2 T.	Vinegar
	Crushed Red Pepper

Clean greens and remove stems. Place in a large pot and cover with water. Add other ingredients. Bring to a boil. Reduce heat and cook until tender (about 2 hours or more). Remove with a slotted spoon. Serves 6-8. These cook down quite a bit.

WHITE BEANS OR BLACK-EYED PEAS (FROM DRIED)

1 lb. bag	Beans or Peas
1 med.	Onion (cut in pieces)
1- 4 oz. Piece	Hog Jowl or Country Bacon
1 T.	Salt
	Black Pepper
	Crushed Red Pepper

Sort and soak beans or peas for several hours in a large pot. Drain and place back in pot. Cover with water. Add other ingredients. Bring to a boil, then reduce heat and cook slowly until tender. Add more seasoning if needed. Spoon into a serving bowl with a slotted spoon. Serves 6-8.

BROCCOLI RING

2 boxes	Frozen Chopped Broccoli
3	Eggs (beaten)
½ t.	Salt
¼ t.	Cayenne Pepper
3 T.	Butter
3 T.	Flour
1 c.	Milk
¾ c.	Mayonnaise
1 t.	Worcestershire Sauce

Cook broccoli in salted water as directed, and drain thoroughly, then mash. In a sauce pan place butter and flour and heat on low. Stir until mixture thickens, then slowly add milk until mixture thickens. Add broccoli, eggs, Worcestershire, salt and pepper to sauce mixture. Fold in mayonnaise. Pour into a well-greased 8" mold. Place mold into a pan ¼ full of water. Bake at 350° about 45 minutes until firm. Serves 8.

BAKED BEANS

2 lg. cans	Pork and Beans or Baked Beans (drained)
1 med.	Onion (chopped)
2/3 c.	Dark Brown Sugar
3 T.	Ketchup
1 T.	Yellow Mustard
1 T.	Worcestershire Sauce
	Salt and Pepper to taste

Pour well drained beans into a baking dish. Mix in other ingredients. Bake at 350° for 30 to 45 minutes until beans are no longer runny. Stir occasionally. Serves 10-12.

STEWED OKRA

1 lb.	Fresh Okra
3 T.	Butter
1 T.	Vinegar
	Salt and Pepper to taste

Clean okra and cut off the tops. Place in a saucepan of water. Add vinegar, salt and pepper. Bring to a boil, then simmer covered until okra starts to become tender. Place butter in a serving bowl, and spoon okra into the bowl. Mix and serve. Serves 4-6.

We call this "slimy okra," but it's really good.

FRIED OKRA

½ lb.	Fresh Okra
2	Eggs
3 T.	Water
½ c.	Flour
1 c.	Corn Meal
½ t.	Salt
¼ t.	Pepper

Clean okra, and cut off tops, then cut into about ¾ inch pieces. Put into a bowl of cold water for a couple of minutes. Drain in a colander. Make an egg wash with the 2 beaten eggs and 3 T. of water. Put okra, a handful at a time in egg wash. Mix flour, corn meal, salt and pepper. Remove okra from egg wash and roll in corn meal. Place in a skillet with heated vegetable or corn oil, and fry until golden brown. Drain on a paper towel.

FRIED GREEN TOMATOES

4-5 medium	Green tomatoes
1 c.	Flour
1 c.	Corn meal
2	Eggs
2 T.	Water
	Crisco or corn oil
	Salt and Pepper

Slice tomatoes and place in a bowl of cold water. Season flour with salt and pepper in a shallow bowl. In another bowl beat eggs and add 2 T. of water. Then in another bowl, put corn meal with salt and pepper seasoning. Slice by slice, coat tomatoes with flour, then dip them in egg wash, and finally in corn meal. Fry in a skillet in oil until brown on both sides. Serve immediately with a sauce. Serves 8-10.

BAKED ONION CASSEROLE

3 medium	Sweet Onions (sliced)
8 oz.	Fresh Sliced Mushrooms
3 T.	Butter
1 c.	Grated Monterey Jack and Colby Cheese
1 can	Cream of Mushroom Soup
1 – 5oz. can	Evaporated Milk
1 t.	Soy Sauce
1 t.	Worcestershire Sauce
6-8 slices	French Bread
6-8 slices	Swiss Cheese
	Cayenne Pepper
	Paprika

In a large skillet, sauté onions and mushrooms in butter over medium-high heat. Spoon into a 2-quart casserole. Sprinkle with the grated cheese. Mix soup, evaporated milk, soy sauce, Worcestershire sauce and cayenne in a small bowl. Pour mixture over the onions and cheese. Arrange the French bread over this, and top with the Swiss cheese. Cover and refrigerate for 4 hours to overnight. Bake, loosely covered at 375° for 30 minutes. Uncover and sprinkle with paprika. Cook an additional 15 to 20 minutes until bubbly. Let set for 5 minutes before serving. Serves 8-12.

When I'm taking this to a tailgate or place where people may not have a knife, I'll cut the bread into bite size pieces.

Remember: Do not put a cold casserole dish into a hot oven. I usually let it set out a while before baking, and even heat in the microwave for about 1 minute.

Seafood

SHRIMP DELIGHT

2 lb.	Shrimp
½ lg.	Green Bell Pepper
½ lg.	Mild Onion
1 small	Clove Garlic
2 stalks	Celery
2 T.	Parsley
1 pt.	Mayonnaise
2 T.	Durkee's Sauce
2 T.	Worcestershire Sauce
1 T.	Lemon Juice
¼ t.	Salt
½ t.	Sugar
½ t.	Tabasco

Cook, peel and de-vein shrimp. In a blender or processor mix bell pepper, onion, garlic, celery, and parsley until almost liquefied. Mix in other ingredients. Marinate shrimp in this mixture overnight. Serve over crisp iceberg lettuce and garnish with quartered tomatoes, hard-boiled eggs, and avocado. Serves 10-12.

This can be used as a side salad (it will serve more than 12), or a main dish salad. We love to make it at the beach. We usually reserve some of the sauce for my sisters, who don't like shrimp, to use over their salad. This is one of the recipes that friends are always asking for, and one of the reasons for writing this book.

This came from a friend of my grandmother, Sallie Byrd Lawrence, a true Southern Lady from Virginia.

CREOLE SHRIMP

1 lb.	Cooked Shrimp
2 T.	Butter
2 T.	Flour
1 small	Onion
5	Stuffed Olives (sliced)
1 can	Tomatoes
1 t.	Parsley
1 t.	Horseradish
2 small cans	Sliced Mushrooms
1 t.	Worcestershire
1 c.	Celery (chopped)
¼ t.	Paprika
¾ c.	Chicken Stock
1 T.	Tomato Paste
1	Green Bell Pepper (chopped)
	Salt and Pepper to taste

Melt butter, add flour, and onions. Cook until onions are slightly browned. Stir in remaining ingredients except mushrooms and shrimp. Simmer slowly for about 20 minutes. Add mushrooms. Add shrimp and cook about 10 minutes. Serve over buttered rice. Serves 6-8.

DEVILED OYSTERS

1 qt.	Oysters (drained)
1 ½ c.	Celery (chopped)
2 T.	Onion (chopped)
1 ½ sticks	Butter
1 t.	Salt
½ t.	Pepper
2 T.	Worcestershire Sauce
2 T.	Lemon Juice
	Tabasco
3 c.	Coarse Bread Crumbs

Melt butter, and add all ingredients except oysters and bread crumbs. Cook mixture until onion and celery are done. In a baking dish (1 ½ to 2 qt.) layer oysters, celery & onion mixture with juices, and bread crumbs. Repeat until all is used. Top with bread crumbs, pats of butter, and sprinkle with black pepper. Pour a small amount of milk around the edge. Bake 20-30 minutes at 400°.

This is a dish we serve every Thanksgiving and Christmas. Some people call it Oyster Dressing.

Nana, my grandmother, taught me how to make this, and the family members who like oysters are glad she did.

CRAB IMPERIAL

1 lb.	Cooked Crab Meat
2 T.	Chopped Onion
2 T.	Chopped Green Bell Pepper
2 T.	Chopped Green Onion
1 T.	Chopped Parsley
1 t.	Dry Mustard
½ t.	Worcestershire Sauce
3 T.	Butter Melted
½ t.	Salt
1 T.	Lemon Juice
2	Eggs (beaten)
1½ c.	White Sauce (see recipe: Sauces)
	Cayenne Pepper to taste

TOPPING:

½ to ¾ c.	Bread Crumbs
2-3 T.	Melted Butter

Mix ingredients and place in individual baking shells or 1½ to 2 qt. baking dish. Top with melted butter and bread crumbs. Bake at 350° for 20-30 minutes until bubbly. Keep in mind that if using shells, it won't take as long for these to cook.

BOILED SHRIMP

2-3 lbs.	Fresh Uncooked Shrimp
1-2	Lemons
1 bag	Shrimp/Crab Boil

Fill a large pot halfway full of water. Squeeze lemons into the water and drop in. Add Crab boil. Bring mixture to a boil and add shrimp (unpeeled). Cook for about 5 minutes until shrimp is pink. Remove from heat, and drain in a colander. Cover with ice, and start peeling when cool enough to handle, or serve chilled and let everyone peel their own. Serve with cocktail sauce.

I rarely use cooked frozen shrimp for anything I fix, they seem to be tough to me. When I have had to use them, I will cook them once they have thawed in this mixture for a couple of minutes.
Another thing is that I don't use those huge shrimp. I think they are tough as well. I usually buy the medium (30-40 count).

Miss Polly's Fried Fish or Shrimp

Desired amount of Fish or Shrimp
Flour seasoned with Salt and Pepper
Beaten Eggs
Japanese Bread Crumbs

Soak fish or peeled shrimp in salted cold water for a short while. Roll in flour mixture, then dip in egg. Cover well with bread crumbs. Fry in a fryer using peanut oil until pieces are well browned and floating at the top of the fryer. With fish, this usually takes about 10 minutes or a little longer. The shrimp will take a shorter amount of time.

Miss Polly's Shrimp & Grits

1 lb.	Fresh Cooked Shrimp
3 c.	Water
1 c.	Whipping Cream
4 T.	Butter
1 t.	Salt
1 c.	Quick Grits
1 c.	Extra Sharp Cheddar Cheese (grated)
2 cloves	Garlic (minced)
1 t.	Worcestershire Sauce
	Cayenne Pepper

Cook, peel and devein shrimp. In a large saucepan bring water, cream, butter and salt to a boil over medium-high heat. Reduce heat to medium and whisk in grits. Cook, stirring constantly for 7-8 minutes. Add Worcestershire, cheese, garlic, shrimp and cayenne pepper. Cook and additional 2-3 minutes until thoroughly heated. Garnish with chives. Serves 10-12.

Note: Remember when serving shellfish to make sure that none of your guests are allergic. At cocktail parties, we label the shellfish dish to avoid confusion.

Miss Polly's Shrimp & Sausage Boil

6 qt.	Water
¾ c.	Old Bay Seasoning
1 t.	Worcestershire sauce
1	Lemon
2 lb.	New red potatoes
2 lb.	Hot smoked sausage links cut into 2" pieces
12 ears	Corn – husked, cleaned and quartered
4 lb.	Large fresh shrimp – unpeeled
	Salt and pepper to taste

Bring water and Old Bay seasoning to a boil in a large stockpot. Cut lemon in half and squeeze into water then drop both halves into the pot. Add Worcestershire sauce, salt and pepper. Add potatoes and cook 5 minutes, then add sausage and cook 5 more minutes. Add corn and cook for 5 minutes, then stir in shrimp and cook until they are pink – about 5 minutes. Drain immediately and serve. Serves 12 – 15.

Add a salad and French bread to this, and you have a meal.

Note: I know that it seems like Miss Polly has a lot of recipes in here, but because she lives in Florida, she has some wonderful seafood recipes, and has allowed me to share them.

GRILLED SALMON

6-8   Salmon Fillets (4-6 oz. Each)
4 T.   Olive oil
4 T.   Lemon Juice
        Sprigs of Dill
        Paprika

Place salmon fillets in a baking dish and drizzle olive oil and lemon over them. Place a sprig of dill on each fillet and sprinkle with paprika. Let them set in this mixture for at least 30 minutes in a cool place. Refrigerate if necessary. Cook these fillets on a medium grill with the skin side down (don't turn) for about 15 minutes, or until they are cooked to desired way. Serves 6-8.

This is obviously a wonderful main dish, but is great over a salad.

GRILLED YELLOW FIN TUNA

1 – 8oz.   Fresh Yellow Fin Tuna Fillet
           Sesame Sauce (see recipe: Sauces)

Place tuna and sauce in a leak proof food bag, and marinate in the refrigerator at least 30 minutes. Place on a hot grill, and reduce heat to medium (if possible). Cook to desired level of doneness.

TUNA CASSEROLE

1 can	Tuna (drain well)
1 can	Cut Asparagus or Party Peas (drained)
1 can	Cream of Mushroom Soup
½ c.	Sour Cream
1 T.	Lemon Juice
2 T.	Butter
1 small pkg.	Wide Egg Noodles (cooked and drained)
	Salt and Pepper to taste
	Breadcrumbs

Cook egg noodles and drain in a colander. Melt 1T. of butter in a baking dish (1½ to 2 qt.). In a bowl, place tuna and lemon. Add soup and sour cream and mix. Add vegetable, salt and pepper, and fold in noodles. Pour into baking dish and top with breadcrumbs and 1 T. melted butter. Bake at 350° for about 30 minutes.

SHRIMP & LOBSTER SALAD

4 c.	Cooked Shrimp and Lobster
1 c.	Celery (chopped)
4	Hard Boiled Eggs (chopped)
2 T.	Lemon Juice
1 c.	Mayonnaise
1 t.	Durkee's Sauce
	Salt and Pepper to taste

Cut shrimp and lobster to bit sized pieces. Add celery, eggs, and some salt and pepper. Mix mayonnaise, durkees, and lemon juice, then fold into mixture. Chill and serve on lettuce. Garnish with tomatoes and avocados. Serves 8-10.

Seafood in White Wine Sauce

½ stick	Butter
4 oz.	Fresh Mushrooms – diced
1/3 c.	Green Onion – chopped
½ t.	Season Salt
½ t.	Black Pepper
2 lg. cloves	Garlic – crushed
½ lb.	Peeled Medium Shrimp
½ lb.	Bay Scallops
6 oz.	Crab
3 T.	Flour
1½ c.	Half and Half
1 c.	Shredded Swiss Cheese
½ c.	White Wine
	Grated Parmesan Cheese
	Chopped Parsley
	Cooked Pasta

Melt butter in a large skillet. Add mushrooms and onions and sauté for about 2 minutes. Add salt, pepper, garlic and seafood and cook another 3 minutes. Add flour, then gradually add half and half that has been heated in the microwave. Add Swiss cheese and cook until it thickens. Stir in white wine. Serve over pasta and top with Parmesan cheese and parsley.

Alternatives: Use only shrimp – 1 ½ lbs. Replace seafood with 1 ½ lbs. of cut up chicken breast. If using chicken, cook for about 5-6 minutes instead of three.
Or for a vegetable dish, use cut carrots, zucchini, yellow squash, broccoli or any combination you like. Add about 2 T. of water, cover and cook the vegetables for about 10 minutes, or until most of the water has cooked off.

I got this recipe from my friend Mary May.

Poultry

Poultry

MAMA'S FRIED CHICKEN

Chicken Pieces (white and dark)
Salted Water
Milk
Seasoned Flour
Crisco and Cooking Oil

Clean chicken and place in cold salted water. After soaking pieces 20-30 minutes, soak in a bowl of milk. In a brown paper bag (or plastic bag), pour about 2-3c. of flour seasoned with salt and pepper. Put pieces of chicken in flour a few at a time, and shake well to cover with flour. Place pieces in a hot skillet about half full of Crisco or a combination of Crisco and cooking oil. Brown on each side and reduce heat. Cover and cook. For larger pieces cook covered about 30 minutes, and smaller about 15-20 minutes. Uncover and increase heat. Cook until golden brown and crisp. Remove and place pieces on a paper towel. For gravy, see Sauces and Gravy: Chicken Gravy (page 176).

GRILLED CHICKEN

4-6	Boneless Chicken Breast Halves
4 T.	Butter
1 T.	Lemon Juice
1 t.	Lemon Pepper
½ t.	Salt
¼ t.	Pepper

Melt butter in a cooking pan on top of the stove. Add other seasonings, then chicken. Turn to low heat and keep on the stove about 20 minutes. Turn the chicken occasionally. Remove from the stove and place the pieces of chicken on a hot to medium grill. Cook an additional 20 minutes. Serves 4-6.
6-8 pieces

BAKED CHICKEN AND RICE

1	Chicken (cut up)
	or
6	Chicken Breast Halves
6 T.	Butter
1 ½ c.	Rice
1½ -2 c.	Water
	Salt and Pepper

Melt butter in a baking dish. Add chicken, and sprinkle each piece with salt and pepper. Cook in the oven at 350° for 20-25 minutes. Add water, make sure it is not cold, and then stir in rice. Cook about 15-20 minutes until rice is done. Stir occasionally. If necessary add more water. Serves 6.

CHICKEN DIVAN

6	Boneless Skinless Chicken Breast Halves
2-10 oz. Boxes	Frozen Broccoli Florets
1 can	Cream of Chicken Soup
1 c.	Sour Cream
¾ c.	Mayonnaise
1 ½ c.	Sharp Cheddar Cheese (grated)
2 T.	Lemon Juice
2 T.	Butter
	Salt and Pepper
	Cayenne Pepper
	Parmesan Cheese

Preheat oven to 350°. Melt butter in 3 qt. casserole dish. Remove from oven and add chicken. Sprinkle each piece with salt and pepper. Cook in oven about 30 minutes. Cook broccoli according to directions, and drain in a colander. In a sauce pan mix soup, sour cream, mayonnaise, lemon juice, and 1c. cheddar cheese. Heat on medium low until cheese has melted. Add some cayenne pepper. Remove chicken dish from oven. Add broccoli, and then cover with sauce. Sprinkle top with ½ c. cheddar cheese and Parmesan. Bake at 350° for an additional 30 minutes. Serves 6.

When I fix this for a crowd where they might not have a knife, I cut the chicken in small pieces before cooking it. It will shorten the time it takes for the chicken to get done.

BAKED CHICKEN SALAD

2 c.	Chicken (cooked and cut in pieces)
2 c.	Celery (chopped)
½ can	Water Sliced Chestnuts
1 small can	Sliced Mushroom
3 T.	Onion (grated)
3 T.	Lemon Juice
1 can	Cream of Chicken Soup
¾ c.	Mayonnaise
½ t.	Salt
½ t.	Pepper

TOPPING:

2 T.	Butter
	Breadcrumbs

In a large bowl mix soup, mayonnaise, lemon juice, onion, salt and pepper. Fold in chicken, water chestnuts, celery, and mushrooms. Pour into a 3 qt. casserole dish. Top with breadcrumbs and melted butter. Bake at 350° for 40 minutes. Serves 10-12.

Serve this over rice or by itself.

Baked Chicken Salad

CHICKEN ARTICHOKE CASSEROLE

4 c.	Cooked Chicken
1 can	Artichoke Hearts (chopped)
1 can	Sliced Mushrooms
1½ c.	Sour Cream
1 can	Cream of Chicken Soup
¾ c.	Mayonnaise
3 T.	Lemon Juice
	Salt and Pepper
	Cayenne Pepper
TOPPING:	
2 T.	Melted Butter
	Breadcrumbs

In a sauce pan over medium low heat mix soup, sour cream, mayonnaise, lemon juice and cayenne pepper. Cut chicken into pieces. Mix chicken, artichoke hearts, and mushrooms in a large bowl, add sauce mixture. Salt and pepper to taste. Pour into a 3 qt. casserole. Top with breadcrumbs and melted butter. Bake at 350° for 30 – 45 minutes until bubbly.
Serves 10-12.

This is another dish that is good with rice or it can stand alone.

EASY CHICKEN TETRAZINI

6 c.	Chicken (cut in bite-size pieces)
8 oz.	Spaghetti or linguini
1 can	Cream of Mushroom Soup
¾ c.	Milk
1 t.	Worcestershire Sauce
2 T.	Pimentos or Chopped Ripe Olives (optional)
1 c.	Sharp Cheddar Cheese (grated)
	Salt and Pepper
	Parmesan Cheese

Cook chicken in pot with water, salt and pepper until done (about 1½ hrs.). Remove from pot and reserve broth. Cook pasta in chicken broth until tender and drain in a colander. Cut chicken into small pieces. Blend soup and milk in a pot, then add chicken and pimentos (if using). Heat thoroughly. Layer pasta, chicken mixture and cheese in a casserole. Sprinkle with salt and pepper. Repeat. Top with cheddar and parmesan cheese. Cover and at 350° for 30-35 minutes.

This is great comfort food, freezes well, and is good to take to people.

CHICKEN CASSEROLE #1

3 c.	Chicken (cooked and cut in pieces)
2 c.	Rice (cooked)
1 bag	Chopped Broccoli (cooked)

SAUCE:

1 can	Cream of Chicken Soup
¾ c.	Sour Cream
½ c.	Mayonnaise
1 T.	Lemon Juice
1 c.	Sharp Cheddar Cheese (grated)
	Parmesan Cheese

Mix soup, sour cream, mayonnaise, lemon juice and ¾ c. of cheese. Heat in a sauce pan until cheese melts. In a casserole layer chicken, rice, and broccoli. Pour sauce over this, and sprinkle remaining cheddar cheese and Parmesan on top. Bake at 325° for 30 minutes. Serves 6-8.

CHICKEN IN NOODLES
& WINE SAUCE

3 c.	Chicken (cooked and cut in pieces)
1-8 oz. Box	Fresh Mushrooms
1 pkg.	Wide Egg Noodles (cooked)
1 can	Cream of Chicken Soup
1 can	Cream of Mushroom Soup
1 jar	Kraft Pimento Cheese
1 T.	Worcestershire Sauce
¼ t.	Onion Juice
½ c.	Sherry
	Salt and Pepper

Mix soups, cheese, Worcestershire, and onion juice in a sauce pan. Heat thoroughly. Add chicken and noodles. Season with wine, salt and pepper. Serves 6-8.

CHICKEN CASSEROLE #2

6-8	Boneless, Skinless Chicken Breasts
1 bunch	Celery Tops
2 c.	Sour Cream
2 cans	Cream of Chicken Soup
1 c.	Chicken Broth
2 t.	Butter
	Breadcrumbs
	Poppy Seeds
	Salt and Pepper

Cook chicken and celery tops in a large pot of water seasoned with salt and pepper until tender (about 1 hour). Cut cooked chicken in large bite size pieces. Strain 1c. of chicken broth from pot. Mix sour cream, soup and broth. Add chicken. Salt and pepper to taste. Pour into a greased 3qt casserole. Top with breadcrumbs, poppy seeds and melted butter. Cook at 300 about 30 minutes until bubbly. Serves 10-12.

Serve this with rice or noodles.

CHICKEN WITH PESTO LINGUINI

2 T.	Olive Oil
1 lb.	Skinless, Boneless Chicken
3	Green Onions (sliced)
1/3 c.	Chopped Pecans (toasted)
1 T.	Garlic (minced)
1/8 t.	Crushed Red Pepper
½ c.	Pesto Sauce
12 oz.	Linguini
¼ c. + 1 T.	Fresh Cilantro (chopped)
¼ c. + 1 T.	Parsley (chopped)
	Salt and Pepper

Cut chicken into thin strips (about 1/3 inch). Heat oil in a large heavy skillet over medium high heat. Season chicken with salt and pepper. Add chicken to oil and sauté for 3-5 minutes. Remove chicken from skillet with a slotted spoon and place in a bowl. In skillet add green onions, garlic, pecans, cilantro and parsley. Sauté for about 2-3 minutes. Add pesto and chicken with any juice from chicken. Stir to blend, then remove from heat. Cook linguini in a large pot of boiling salted water. Reserve ¼ to ½ c. of the water. Drain linguini. Bring sauce and chicken to a simmer, add linguini and water, and mix well to coat. Salt and pepper to taste. Serves 6-8.

Meat

Meat

BEEF TENDERLOIN

Beef Tenderloin - 4-6 lbs.
Garlic Cloves or Powder
Salt and Pepper
Splash of Worcestershire Sauce
Splash of Vinegar

Place tenderloin in an aluminum pan. Sprinkle with salt and pepper. Add garlic, and then splash on a little Worcestershire sauce and vinegar. Put in the oven at 500° for 23 minutes. Remove from oven and wrap in heavy aluminum foil, and place in a styrofoam cooler until ready to serve. The tenderloin will continue to cook in the cooler, so the longer it's left in there, the more done it will become. It may sound crazy, but it works. If it doesn't get done enough, run it back in the oven at 350° for a few minutes.

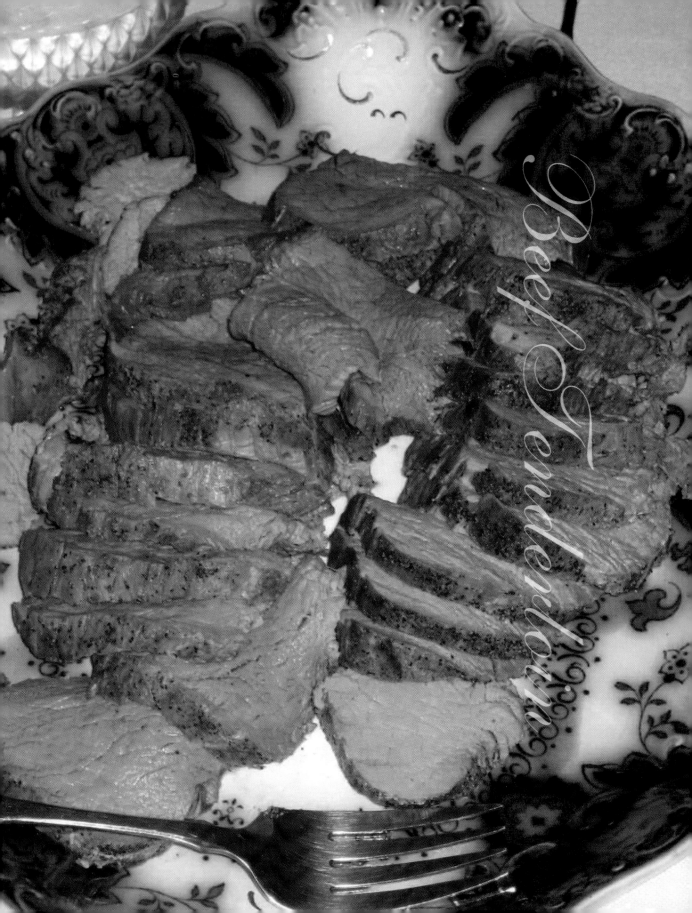

Beef Tenderloin

EYE OF ROUND ROAST

Eye of Round Roast
Salt and Pepper
Garlic Powder

Rub roast with salt, pepper, and garlic powder. Place in a baking pan, and then cook in a 500° oven for 5 minutes. Turn oven off after 5 minutes and let roast remain until oven cools.

COUNTRY FRIED STEAK

4-6	**Minute Steaks**
2 T.	**Butter**
2 T.	**Flour**
1 c.	**Water**
1 t.	**Kitchen Bouquet**
	Salt and Pepper

Melt butter in a large skillet, and add minute steaks. Sprinkle with salt and pepper. Brown on each side and remove from skillet. Add flour to butter. If much of the butter has been absorbed by the steaks, add a little more before putting the flour in the skillet. Once the flour and butter are mix thoroughly, begin to add water, salt and pepper, and Kitchen Bouquet. Mix thoroughly and bring to a boil. Return steaks to the skillet. Cover and simmer about 20 minutes. The gravy around the steaks should be fairly thick. If not, make a thickener with flour or cornstarch and a little water, and slowly add it into the gravy. Serves 4-6.

PULL APART
(POT ROAST)

2-3 lb.	Beef Roast
2-3 med.	Onions
1 1/2 lbs.	Baby Carrots
3-4	Potatoes
1 T.	Vinegar
1 T.	Worcestershire Sauce
	Salt and Pepper
	Water

GRAVY:

3 T.	Ketchup
2 T.	Chili Sauce
1 T.	Worcestershire Sauce
	Splash of Vinegar

Place roast in a roasting pan. Sprinkle with salt and pepper. Add vinegar and Worcestershire sauce. Cook in a 350° oven until roast is brown. Remove from the oven and cover with water. Add onions that have been cut in half. Cook another 20 minutes and add cut up potatoes. Cook another 20 minutes and add baby carrots. Then cook until carrots are tender. To make the gravy, remove roast and vegetables, and add the gravy ingredients. If gravy is not thick enough, mix a little flour or cornstarch in just a little water. Pour some of this into the gravy until it thickens. Serves 6-8.

OLD TIME BEEF HASH

1-1½ lbs.	Left Over Roast
½ med.	Onion (chopped)
2-3	Potatoes (cubed)
½ T.	Worcestershire Sauce
	Salt and Pepper to taste

Cut left over roast (either eye of round or tenderloin) into bit size pieces. In a large skillet cook onion in water, Worcestershire Sauce, salt and pepper until tender. Add cubed potatoes and cook until they are tender (about 10-15 minutes). Add beef and cook until all the flavors have blended together. About 15 minutes. If necessary add some Kitchen Bouquet for additional color. Serves 4-6. This is great served over cornbread cakes (see: Breads).

My mother calls this Old Time Depression Hash, because during the Depression they would serve dishes like this from their leftovers, if they were fortunate enough to even be able to buy a roast for Sunday dinner.

MEAT LOAF

2 lbs.	Ground Chuck or Round
½ c.	Onion (chopped)
1	Egg
1 T.	Worcestershire Sauce
1 t.	Vinegar
1 can	Creole Sauce
1 t.	Salt
½ t.	Pepper

In a large bowl mix onion, egg, Worcestershire sauce, vinegar, salt, pepper, and about ½ of the can of Creole sauce with meat. It's best to mix this with your hands. Form a loaf, and place in a baking dish in a 350° oven. Cook about 30 minutes, then remove. Skim off any excess grease, and pour the rest of the Creole sauce over the meat loaf. Return to the oven and cook an additional 30 minutes. Serves 6-8.

My son, Perry, just decided about a year ago that he likes meat loaf, and now wants it all the time, as do his friends.

MEAT SAUCE FOR SPAGHETTI OR LASAGNA

1 ½ to 2 lbs.	Ground Beef or Chuck
½ lg.	Onion – diced
2 cloves	Garlic
3 – 14.5 oz. cans	Tomatoes
3 – 8 oz. cans	Tomato Sauce
1 12 oz. can	Tomato Paste
½ t.	Chopped Parsley
½ t.	Chopped Basil
½ t.	Chopped Oregano
2	Bay Leaves
¼ t.	Chili Powder
¼ t.	Crushed Red pepper
1 T.	Vinegar
1 T.	Worcestershire Sauce
½ t.	Salt
¼ t.	Black pepper

Mix ingredients in a large pot and simmer at least one hour. The longer, the better within reason say 2-3 hours. Stir occasionally so it doesn't stick. Use over spaghetti, other pastas, or as the meat sauce in lasagna.

GRILLED TARRAGON PORK CHOPS

4-6   Grilling Style Pork Chops
4 T.   Butter
2 T.   Fresh or Dried Tarragon
       Salt and Pepper

In a baking pan on the stove top, melt butter. Add tarragon, salt and pepper. Place chops in this mixture and cook and marinate on the stove 15-20 minutes. Then place on a medium hot grill and cook an additional 20-30 minutes. Serves 4-6.

SOUTHERN FRIED PORK CHOPS

Center Cut Pork Chops
Flour
Salt and Pepper

Season flour with salt and pepper. Roll chops in flour mixture until coated. Place in a skillet with hot oil or Crisco. Brown on both sides, then reduce heat and cover. Cook about 15-20 minutes. Uncover and increase heat. Cook on both sides until crisp.

PORK ROAST

3-4 lb.   Pork Loin
          Salt and Pepper

GRAVY:

          Drippings
¼ c.   Chili Sauce
1 T.   Dark Brown Sugar
1 T.   Worcestershire Sauce
          Water
          Salt and Pepper

Sprinkle salt and pepper over pork loin, and place in a 350° oven. Cook 1-1½ hr. until tender. Top will be good and crusty. Remove from pan. Place pan with drippings on the stovetop on medium heat. Add water and other ingredients. Cook until the gravy has thickened a little. Serves 10-12.

PORK TENDERLOIN

2 – 1 ½ -2lb.   Pork Tenderloins

Marinade for Pork (page 175)

Place tenderloins in a sealable plastic bag with marinade. Refrigerate at least 4 hours. Overnight is really better. Remove tenderloins from bag and cook on a medium hot grill for about 1 hour until done. Turn several times, so that all sides are browned. These can be cooked in the oven (probably 350°), but are much better on the grill.

BAKED HAM

2-3 lb.   **Fully Cooked Boneless Ham**
½ c.   **Coca Cola**

OPTIONAL:

Cloves

Place ham in heavy aluminum foil and put it in a baking pan. Pour Coke over ham, and tent foil. Cook in 325° oven for 15-20 minutes per pound.

We don't do a lot with ham. When we do, we don't usually get ham that has to be cooked, but will always cook even a fully cooked ham for a while. The Coke just adds to the flavor, and makes it a little more tender.

LEG OF LAMB

3-4 lb.   Leg of Lamb (butterflied)

MARINADE FOR LAMB (see: Marinades recipe page 179)

¾ c.   Dijon Mustard
1 T.   Fresh or Dried Rosemary

Place lamb in a sealable plastic bag with marinade. Refrigerate overnight it possible.
Mix mustard and rosemary. Remove lamb from bag and brush on one side with mustard
mixture. Place on a medium hot grill with mustard side down. Brush top with mustard mixture.
Cook 20-30 minutes on each side. Brush again with mustard if needed. Serves 10-12.

This will work for lamb chops or rack of lamb as well.

My uncle, Jimmie introduced us to this recipe for lamb. We use it every Easter.

Sauces, Gravies & Marinades

Sauces, Gravies & Marinades

CHOCOLATE SAUCE

1 c.	Sugar
2 T.	Cocoa
1 T.	Flour
1 c.	Milk
1 t.	Vanilla
2 T.	Butter

Mix sugar, cocoa, and flour in a saucepan. Stir in milk, and bring to a boil. Add vanilla and butter, and remove from the heat.

JANE'S CARAMEL SAUCE

1 c.	White Sugar
1 c.	Light Karo Syrup
1 stick	Margarine or Butter

Bring this mixture to a boil. In a skillet caramelize ¼ cup of sugar and add it to this mixture and blend. Let this cool a little, then add ½ pint of whipping cream. Boil for 3 minutes. This sauce keeps very well in the refrigerator.

This recipe is from our family friend Jane, who was recently taken from us.

Jezebel Sauce

10 oz. jar   Apple Jelly
10 oz. jar   Pineapple Preserves
8 oz. jar   Yellow Mustard
1 t.   Dry Mustard
1 t.   Vinegar
4-5 oz.   Horseradish

Mix all ingredients and heat until everything is blended.

This sauce will keep in the refigerator for weeks and is wonderful with chicken tenders.

HOLLANDAISE SAUCE

5 oz.	Butter
6	Egg Yolks
2 T.	Lemon Juice
½ t.	Salt
	Cayenne Pepper to taste
¼ c.	Ice Water

Melt butter in a double boiler at a low temperature. Try not to bring the water to a boil. In a bowl, whisk egg yolks, lemon juice, salt and cayenne pepper until the mixture turns a bright yellow. Add ice water, and mix. Pour mixture into double boiler and whisk until it thickens (about 10-15 minutes).

Good over asparagus, broccoli, or eggs benedict.

WHITE SAUCE

2 T.   **Butter**
2 T.   **Flour**
1 c.   **Milk or Cream**
       Salt and Pepper to taste

Melt butter in a saucepan, and add flour. Mix until thoroughly blended, and then begin to add milk a little at a time over a medium low heat. Stir until the mixture thickens. Add salt and pepper.

This is just a good basic sauce. You can add cheese to make a cheese sauce. Some recipes just call for a white sauce.

MARINADE FOR PORK TENDERLOIN

½ c.	Strong Coffee (cold)
2 T.	Soy Sauce
1 T.	Worcestershire Sauce
1 T.	Vinegar
2 cloves	Garlic
½ c.	Italian Dressing

Mix ingredients in a gallon size kitchen bag, and add tenderloin (one or two). Refrigerate several hours (overnight if possible).

I've only used this for pork tenderloin. I guess it would be good for grilling pork chops, or even chicken. Use your imagination.

CHICKEN GRAVY

3-4 T.	Seasoned Flour
1 c.	Milk
	Drippings from Fried Chicken

In a skillet, mix flour seasoned with salt and pepper with the drippings from the fried chicken (usually about 2-3 T. of grease) over medium low heat. When this mixture is blended, it will look a little pasty. Begin to add milk slowly, and increase heat a bit. Add more salt and pepper to taste. Bring it to a boil, and remove from heat once it has thickened.

I usually use the left over flour that the chicken was in before it was cooked, as well as the milk in which it has been soaked.

Judy's Marinade

½ c.	Safflower Oil
1/3 c.	Soy Sauce
3 T.	Red Wine Vinegar
½ t.	Garlic Powder
½ t.	Onion Powder

Mix ingredients together. Marinate chicken, pork, steaks, or shrimp several hours or overnight. Baste meats with mixture while grilling.

Tuna Marinade

2 T.   Sesame Oil
2 T.   Soy Sauce
2 T.   Lemon Juice
        Coarse Black Pepper

Mix in a sealable kitchen bag. Add tuna steak and marinate at least 30 minutes before grilling.

LAMB MARINADE

4 cloves	Garlic
2/3 c.	Lemon Juice
1/3 c.	Dry White Vermouth
1 T.	Rosemary
¼ c.	Olive Oil
¼ c.	Worcestershire Sauce
	Salt and Pepper to taste

Mix in a large sealable kitchen bag or covered pan. Add butterflied leg of lamb or lamb chops. Refrigerate over night. See: Lamb recipe.

This along with the lamb recipe came from Jimmie

REMOULADE SAUCE

1 c.	Hellmann's Mayonnaise
¼ c.	Sour Pickle – chopped
1 T.	Capers
½ t.	Mustard
½ t.	Chopped Parsley
1/8 t.	Tarragon
	Horseradish to taste

Mix and chill.
This is great with seafood, especially crab.

MARY'S MANGO SALSA

5 lg.	Tomatoes – assorted red and yellow
2 ripe	Mangos
1 bunch	Fresh Cilantro
1 med.	Red Onion
2-3	Fresh Jalapenos
1	Lime
1	Orange

Core, partially peel and dice tomatoes. Combine with peeled and diced mangos. Add chopped onion, minced cilantro, and diced jalapenos. Squeeze the lime and orange juice over the mixture. Salt to taste and chill. Drain before serving with tortilla chips.

Another from Mary May.

Pickles & Preserves

CHILI SAUCE

4 qts.	Tomatoes (peeled and chopped)
2 c.	Chopped Onions
1 c.	Chopped Sweet Red Pepper
1 c.	Chopped Green Pepper
1 small	Hot Red Pepper
3 T.	Salt
½ c.	Sugar
1 T.	White Mustard Seed
1 t.	Cinnamon
1 t.	Allspice
2 ½ c.	Vinegar

Combine vegetables, salt and sugar. Cook 1-2 hours. Add vinegar and spices. Cook 4-5 hours until thick. Add 2 T. corn starch in water and mix. Pour into sterilized jars and seal.

Chili Sauce

Bell Pepper Jelly

6 c.	Sugar
½ c.	Bell Peppers
1½ c.	Vinegar
½ c.	Hot Peppers
6 oz. jar	Certo
	Green Food Coloring

Grind peppers. Add sugar and vinegar. Bring to a boil. Remove from heat, and let stand for 5 minutes. Add Certo and green food coloring if it's not green enough. Strain and pour into 6 sterilized jelly jars. Seal.

SQUASH PICKLES

6 lbs.	Baby Yellow Squash (thinly sliced)
8 small	Onions (finely chopped)
1	Sweet Red Pepper (thinly sliced)
1	Sweet Green Pepper (thinly sliced)
½ c.	Coarse Salt
	Ice

Place vegetables in a large pan. Sprinkle with coarse salt, and fill the pan with ice cubes. Let stand 3 hours and then drain.

MIX:

4 c.	Sugar
5 c.	White Vinegar
½ t.	Mustard Seed
½ t.	Celery Seed
1½ t.	Turmeric

Heat mixture and pour over drained squash. Heat all until well scalded – just to boiling point. Pour into sterilized jars and seal.

Baby squash can usually be found at the end of the growing season. Early fall.

GREEN TOMATO PICKLES

7 lbs.	Sliced Green Tomato Pickles
	(use small ones)
2 gal.	Water
3 c.	Unslaked Lime

Dissolve unslaked lime in water. Add tomatoes and soak for several hours. Drain and soak in fresh water for 4 hours, changing the water every hour.

MIX IN LARGE KETTLE:

5 lbs.	Sugar
3 pts.	White Vinegar
1 t.	Ginger
1 t.	Allspice
1 t.	Cinnamon
1 t.	Mace
1 t.	Whole Cloves
1 t.	Celery Seed

Add tomatoes to mixture and bring to a boil. Remove from heat and let stand overnight. Bring to a boil and simmer for 1 hour. Put into sterilized jars and seal.

LEMON CURD

½ c.	Butter
½ c.	Fresh Lemon Juice
3 t.	Fresh Lemon Rind
1½ c.	Sugar
5	Eggs (beaten)
1 t.	Vanilla

Melt butter in a saucepan. Add lemon juice, rind and sugar. Cook and stir constantly until sugar dissolves. Add eggs and cook, stirring constantly until mixture thickens. Add vanilla and remove from heat. Allow to cool, then refrigerate.

STRAWBERRY PRESERVES

1 qt.	Strawberries
3 c.	Sugar

Mix 1½ c. sugar with berries in a pot and cook for 5 minutes. Add the rest of the sugar and cook for 10 – 15 minutes. Pour into a crock bowl and let stand for 24 hours. Stir occasionally. Pour into sterilized jelly jars and seal.

Breads & Cakes

Breads & Cakes

CORNBREAD

1	Egg (beaten)
1½ c. +	Buttermilk
½ t.	Baking Soda
1 c.	Corn Meal
¾ c.	Flour
2 t.	Baking Powder
1 t.	Salt
2 T.	Crisco

Dissolve baking soda in buttermilk. Combine other ingredients except for the Crisco (you can use corn or vegetable oil). Melt Crisco in a baking pan, and pour about half of it into the batter. If the batter seems too thick, add a little more buttermilk. Bake in a preheated 450° oven about 20 minutes. If top does not brown, turn on the broiler for a minute or two. Serves 10-12.

Don't cook this too long. You don't want it to dry out.

SPOON BREAD

1 c.	Corn meal
1½ c.	Boiling water
1 T.	Melted butter
3	Eggs
1 c.	Milk
1 t.	Baking powder
1 t.	Salt

Add boiling water to corn meal and allow it to cool. Add beaten eggs and other ingredients, except butter. Melt butter in 2 qt. Pyrex, and pour in mixture.
Bake at 350° for 30 – 40 minutes.

CORNBREAD DRESSING

½ pkg.	Pepperidge Farm Cornbread Stuffing
½ pkg.	Pepperidge Farm Herb Stuffing
2 c.	Crumbled Cornbread
1 c.	Light Bread Crumbs
2 c.	Chopped Celery
1 c.	Chopped Onion
1 c.	Chicken or Turkey Stock
1	Egg (beaten)
1 can	Cream of Celery Soup
1 can	Cream of Onion Soup

Sauté celery and onion in water, then mix with other ingredients in a large bowl. Form into patties and place on a greased baking sheet. Bake for 20-30 minutes in a 400° oven. Serves 12-15. This can be cooked in a baking pan. It will need to cook longer.

CORNBREAD CAKES

1   Egg
½ t.   Baking Soda
1 c.   Corn Meal
1½ c.   Buttermilk
½ t.   Salt

Beat egg. Add soda to buttermilk. Add other ingredients and mix well. If it seems too runny add some more meal. Drop in a hot greased skillet and cook like a pancake.

HOT WATER CORNBREAD

Corn meal

Boiling water

Salt

Pour boiling water over meal and salt and mix together. Spoon into a skillet with about ½" of cooking oil. Cook until brown. Sometimes we chill the batter before cooking.

ELLA'S ROLLS

4 c.	Whole Milk
1 c.	Sugar
1 c.	Crisco
1 cake or 1½ pkg.	Yeast
6½ + ½ c.	All-Purpose Flour
1 T.	Salt
1 t.	Baking Soda
1 T. (heaping)	Baking Powder
2-3 sticks	Melted Butter

Scald milk and pour over sugar and shortening in a large mixing bowl. Cool to lukewarm. Break up yeast into this mixture and stir until it dissolves. Using a hand mixer, add 5 ½ cups of flour until it gets quite thick. Cover and allow to rise 2 hours in a warm place. It will more than double. Add salt, soda and ½ cup of flour. Beat thoroughly using one beater. Add baking powder and remaining cup of flour or as much as needed for dough to be thick, but still wet.

Cover and chill overnight. Remove from refrigerator and work ½ of the dough at a time. Punch down and place ½ on a well floured surface. Use about 1 cup of flour to make the right consistency. Roll out to ¼" thick, and cut with a biscuit cutter. Dip rounds in melted butter and fold in half (pocketbook style). Place side by side on a well-greased jelly roll pan – 5 across and 10 down. Cover lightly and let rise 2 hours. Preheat oven to 350. Bake until lightly brown, about 15 minutes. Cool, wrap and freeze.
Ella says to freeze these in wax paper and aluminum foil in packs of 25. The recipe should make 100 rolls. They will keep indefinitely in the freezer.

To serve, remove wax paper, and place in a 350° oven in foil for about 15 minutes until they have warmed.

For whole wheat rolls use ½ whole wheat flour and ½ white flour.

This is a very extensive process, but you will not believe how delicious these rolls are. I appreciate Ella's allowing me to share this, as I do all who have done the same.

ROLLS

6 c.	Flour
1 c.	Milk (scalded)
1 c.	Cold Water
6 T.	Sugar
2 t.	Salt
2	Eggs (beaten)
6 T.	Crisco
2 cakes	Yeast (or 2 packages)

Measure and sift flour. Put aside. Heat milk to scalding. In a large bowl mix sugar, salt and shortening. Pour in hot milk and stir until ingredients dissolve. Add cold water. Mixture should be neither hot nor cold. Crumble in yeast, and stir until it has dissolved. Add ½ of the flour, then eggs. Add the other ½ of the flour and stir until well mixed. Turn out on a floured board and shape into a large soft ball. Put into a greased, airtight bowl and refrigerate. This will keep in the refrigerator 3-4 days, or it can be shaped into rolls immediately and put to rise. Let rise 1½ to 2 hours. Brush with butter. Bake in a 400°-450° oven until brown, 5 to 10 minutes. Makes several dozen depending on the size of the rolls.

POTATO ROLLS

1 cake	Yeast (or 1 package)
½ c.	Lukewarm Water from Potatoes
1 c.	Milk
½ c.	Melted Shortening
¼ c.	Sugar
2	Eggs (beaten)
1 ½ t.	Salt
½ c.	Mashed Potatoes
4-5 c.	Sifted Flour

Mix ingredients using enough flour to make a soft dough. Place in a bowl in the refrigerator overnight. Make into rolls on a baking sheet and allow to rise in a warm place 2 hours. Brush with butter. Bake in a 400°- 450° oven for 10-12 minutes until brown.

BREAD

5½ c.	Cold Water
2 pkg.	Yeast
2 T.	Salt
1/3 c.	Oil
½ c.	Honey
12 c.	Whole Wheat or Stone Ground Flour

Stir yeast into water until it dissolves. Add salt, oil and honey and stir. Add flour all at once, and stir until mixed. Knead for 5-10 minutes. Lay in a large bowl and cover with plastic wrap. Refrigerate overnight. Remove from refrigerator and let stand ½ hour. Place on floured board and knead for 10 minutes. Cut into 4 pieces and shape into loaves. Place in 4 greased loaf pans. Lightly butter top. Place in 375° oven for 40-50 minutes.

MEXICAN CORNBREAD

2	Eggs
1 c.	Grated Sharp Cheddar Cheese
1 c.	Cream Style Corn
2 oz. jar	Pimentos
½ c.	Oil
¾ c.	Buttermilk
1-3	Jalapenos
1 c.	Corn Meal
1 T.	Flour
1 t.	Salt
½ t.	Baking Soda

Mix ingredients, and pour into a skillet. Brown in the skillet on top of the stove. Bake for 20 minutes at 350° – 375°. Broil for 5 minutes or until brown.

Corn Light Bread

2 c.	Corn Meal (plain)
½ c.	Flour (plain)
½ c.	Sugar
2 c.	Buttermilk
1 t.	Baking Soda (scant)
1	Egg

Mix and pour into a loaf pan. Bake at 400° to 450° oven about 40 minutes, or steam until it rises – about 30 minutes and then brown.

DATE NUT BREAD

1½ c.	Sugar
2¾ c.	Sifted Flour
2 t.	Baking Soda
½ t.	Salt
1 stick	Butter
1½ c.	Boiling Water
1 T.	Vanilla
1 c.	Chopped Pecans
1 box	Chopped Dates
2	Eggs

Pour water over nuts, dates, and butter. In another bowl beat eggs and add sugar. Add to water and date mixture. Add soda, salt and flour. Grease and flour 2 loaf pans. Pour mixture into pans and bake at 350° for 1 hour.

This is great to serve at a luncheon. Spread cream cheese on one piece and top with another piece.

MAMA'S BUTTERMILK CAKE

1 stick	Butter
½ c.	Crisco
3 c.	Sugar
3 c.	Sifted Flour
5	Eggs
½ t.	Baking Soda
1 T.	Boiling Water
1 c.	Buttermilk
1 T.	Vanilla

Dissolve soda in boiling water. Mix all ingredients. Pour batter into two loaf pans that have been greased and floured. Place in a 350° oven for 1 hour or until brown and crusty on top.

Mama's been making these cakes as long as I can remember. When we were young she baked them for all of our teachers as well as many friends. She still is up late at night during Christmas making more than 100 of these delicious loaves. Everyone loves this cake. It is great toasted with butter in the morning in addition to being served by itself, with Lemon Curd topping, or topped with ice cream and strawberries or peaches.

CHESS CAKE

1 box	Dark Brown Sugar
1 c.	Sugar
2 sticks	Butter
4	Eggs
2 c.	Flour
2 t.	Baking Powder
¼ t.	Salt
1 c.	Chopped Pecans
1 t.	Vanilla

Melt butter and add sugar. Separate eggs and beat yolks. Add to butter and sugar. Sift in flour, baking powder and salt. Add pecans. Beat egg whites and fold into mixture. Add vanilla. Pour batter into greased baking pan and bake 30 – 40 minutes at 325˚. Top with powdered sugar, and cut into pieces.

My friends Judy and Mimi love this. I try to fix it for them every Christmas.

FUDGE CAKE

2 sticks	Butter
2 c.	Sugar
2 c.	Flour
8 T.	Cocoa
4	Eggs
1 c.	Chopped Pecans
1½ t.	Vanilla

Cream butter and sugar. Add flour, cocoa, eggs, pecans and vanilla. Pour into a greased pan, and bake in a 375˚ oven for 15 – 20 minutes.

HERSHEY BAR CAKE

8 oz.	Hershey's Chocolate Syrup
8 (5 oz. bars)	Hershey Bars (melted)
2 sticks	Butter or Margarine
2 c.	Sugar
4	Eggs
1 c.	Buttermilk
½ t.	Soda
2½ c.	Flour
1 c.	Chopped Pecans
½ t.	Vanilla

Cream butter and sugar. Add eggs one at a time, beating well after each. Combine soda and milk and set aside for a few minutes. Add flour and milk alternately to mixture. Add melted Hershey bars, syrup, pecans, and vanilla. Pour into a greased tube or bundt pan and bake at 300° for 2 hours.

This is great warm with ice cream and chocolate sauce (See: Sauces).

SOUR CREAM COFFEE CAKE

BATTER:

1 c.	Butter (2 sticks)
2 c.	Sugar
2 c.	Flour
½ t.	Salt
1 t.	Baking Powder
2	Eggs
1 c.	Sour Cream
1 t.	Vanilla

FILLING:

½ c.	Chopped Pecans
2 t.	Ground Cinnamon
3 T.	Dark Brown Sugar (packed)

Mix batter and filling separately. Pour ½ of batter into a greased and floured bundt pan. Sprinkle filling over this. Pour in the other ½ of the batter. Bake at 350° for 60-65 minutes until golden brown.

If you have small bundt pans, you can get two cakes. Remember that you will not have to cook them quite as long.

RED VELVET CAKE

CAKE:

1½ c.	Sugar
½ c.	Crisco
2	Eggs
2½ c.	Cake Flour
1 c.	Buttermilk
2 oz.	Red Food Coloring
2 T.	Cocoa
1 t.	Vanilla
1 t.	Baking Soda
	Pinch of salt

Cream sugar and Crisco. Add while beating well eggs, flour and buttermilk. Add food coloring, cocoa, baking soda, salt and vanilla. Blend thoroughly. Bake in two 9" greased and floured cake pans at 350° for 30 minutes.

ICING:

5 T.	Flour
1 c.	Whole Milk
1 c.	Sugar
1 c.	Butter
1 t.	Vanilla

Make a smooth paste of flour and milk and cook in a double boiler until thick. Remove from heat and allow to cool. Cream sugar, vanilla and butter together in a mixer for 5 minutes. Add this to cold flour and milk mixture and beat in a mixer until creamy.

"Other Mama's" Prune Cake

3	Eggs
1½ c.	Sugar
2 c.	Flour
1 c.	Cooking Oil
4-5 oz.	Stewed Prunes
1 c.	Chopped Dried Prunes
1 c.	Chopped Pecans
½ t.	Salt
1 t.	Cinnamon
1 t.	Nutmeg
1 t.	Allspice
1 t.	Baking Soda
1 c.	Buttermilk
1 t.	Vanilla

Beat eggs, and mix all other ingredients by hand until thoroughly blended. Bake in a greased and floured tube or large flat pan for 45 minutes at 325°.

Spread cake with *Caramel Icing*.

CARAMEL ICING

2 c.	Sugar
1 c.	Buttermilk
2 t.	Corn Syrup
1 c.	Butter
1 t.	Soda
1 t.	Vanilla

Cook until a soft ball will form in a cup of water. Remove from heat and beat until thick enough to spread.

"Other Mama" was my great grandmother. We used to go to her house to eat Sunday dinner. If we weren't at her house, we went to my grandmother's, and now Mama's.

BETTY'S CARAMEL ICING

2 sticks	Butter
3 c.	Sugar
2 c.	Whipping Cream
	(before being whipped)

Place butter, sugar and cream in a heavy bottomed pot on high. Reduce heat to medium and bring to a boil. Remove from heat. In a frying pan put 5-6 heaping tablespoons of sugar on medium heat. Stir to let it get to a rich caramel color. Stir until it turns color and is thoroughly melted. Pour this into the other mixture in a thin stream. Stir over medium heat and cook until the soft ball stage. About 30 minutes. Ice cake once the icing has cooled a little.

ELLEN'S RUM CAKE

1	**Yellow Cake Mix** (Duncan Hines – Tradition)
1 box	**Jell-O Instant Vanilla Pudding**
4	**Eggs**
½ c.	**Mazola Oil**
½ c.	**Light Rum**
½ t.	**Vanilla**

Mix ingredients together well. Pour into greased and floured bundt pan (or 2 small ones). Bake at 350° – 50-55 min. for large pan, or 45 minutes for small. Leave cake in the pan until it cools. Poke holes in the top and pour sauce over it.

Sauce:

1 stick	**Butter**
1 c.	**Sugar**
½ c.	**Water**
1/3 c.	**Light Rum**

Cook this until it boils.

Variation: Instead of rum, use amaretto.

ELLEN'S ALMOND CAKE WITH RASPBERRY SAUCE

¾ c.	Sugar
1 stick	Unsalted Butter (room temperature)
8 oz.	Almond Paste (crumbled)
3	Eggs
2 t.	Triple Sec
½ t.	Almond Extract
¼ c.	Flour
1/3 t.	Baking Powder
	Powdered Sugar
Sauce:	
2 c.	Fresh Raspberries or Strawberries
or	
12 oz.	Frozen Berries – thawed
2 T.	Sugar
1 t.	Triple Sec

Combine sugar, butter and almond paste, beating until well blended. Beat in eggs one at a time, and add the liqueur and extract. Add flour and baking powder, mixing just until it is thoroughly mixed (don't over beat). Pour into an 8 or 9 inch round cake pan that has been well buttered and floured. Bake in preheated 350° oven for 40-45 minutes.
Allow to cool, and invert on serving plate. Sift powdered sugar over the top.

Sauce: Puree the berries and liqueur. Add sugar. Press through sieve to remove seeds if desired. Serve with the cake. Serves 8-10.

This is another specialty from sister Ellen.

Almond Cake with Raspberry Sauce

SOUR CREAM MUFFINS

½ c.	Butter
1 c.	Sugar
2¾ c.	Flour
½ t.	Salt
1 t.	Baking Soda
4	Eggs (beaten)
1½ c.	Sour Cream
1 t.	Vanilla
	Pinch of Nutmeg

Cream butter and sugar until fluffy. Sift in flour, baking soda and salt. Add alternately with the eggs and sour cream, starting and ending with the flour mix. Mix lightly and as little as possible. Pour into 24-30 muffin tins and sprinkle with sugar. Bake at 450° for 15 minutes or until brown

BANANA MUFFINS

2 c.	Flour
1 t.	Baking Soda
1 t.	Baking Powder
¼ c.	Buttermilk
1 stick	Butter
1 c.	Sugar
2	Eggs (beaten)
3	Very Ripe Bananas
½ c.	Pecans
1 t.	Vanilla

Sift dry ingredients together. Cream butter and sugar, and then add dry ingredients. Add beaten eggs. Sieve bananas and add to mixture. Stir in buttermilk. Add pecans and vanilla. Bake in greased muffin tins at 400° for about 20 minutes or until brown.

CARROT CAKE

2 c.	Sugar
2 c.	Flour
1½ t.	Baking Soda
1½ t.	Salt
2 t.	Cinnamon
1½ c.	Vegetable Oil
4	Eggs (beaten)
2 c.	Grated Carrots
2 c.	Chopped Pecans
1 t.	Vanilla

Mix dry ingredients together. Add oil. Stir well. Add eggs and stir well. Add carrots, nuts and vanilla. Bake in three 9" cake pans or 1 sheet cake pan that have been greased and floured at 350° for 25 minutes. Can make into muffins.

Top with a cream cheese icing if desired.

APRICOT-LEMON CAKE

1 box	Lemon Supreme Cake Mix (Duncan Hines)
¾ c.	Vegetable Oil
2/3 c.	Apricot Nectar
1/3 c.	Apricot Preserves
2	Eggs (beaten)
½ c.	Sugar

Mix and pour into a greased tube pan. Bake at 325° for 1 hour. Cool partially and remove from pan. Then glaze while still warm.

GLAZE:

1	Lemon (juiced)
½ c.	Apricot Nectar
1T.	Apricot Preserves
1-1 ½ c.	Powdered Sugar

Mix well and pour over cake.

STRAWBERRY CAKE

1 box	White Cake Mix
3 T.	Flour (sifted)
1 box	Strawberry Jell-O
½ c.	Strawberries (mashed up)
4	Eggs (beaten)
1 c.	Vegetable Oil
½ c.	Milk
1 t.	Vanilla

Mix all together. If using frozen strawberries, be sure to thaw them. If using fresh, add 2 T. of sugar, and let dissolve over berries. Bake in a greased and floured bundt pan or sheet cake pan at 350° for about 45 minutes. Allow to partially cool, then remove from pan and ice.

ICING:

½ c.	Strawberries (mashed up)
1 stick	Butter
1 box	Powdered Sugar

Cream butter and sugar, and beat until fluffy, then add strawberries.

INDIVIDUAL CHEESE CAKES

STEP 1:

3 – 8oz. pkgs.	Cream Cheese
5	Eggs
1 c.	Sugar
1 ½ t.	Vanilla

STEP 2:

½ pt.	Sour Cream
½ c.	Sugar
1 t.	Vanilla
	Strawberry & Apricot Preserves

Mix ingredients in step 1, and pour into cupcake papers ½ full. Bake 30 – 40 minutes at 300˚. Remove and allow to cool completely. Mix step 2 ingredients except preserves and spoon about 1 teaspoon on top. Top with a spoonful of preserves. Place in oven another 5 minutes. Yield about 3 dozen.

I usually make these in the mini cupcake papers, and get almost twice as many. You can use whatever kinds of preserves you like, but these are really good.

NUT BREAD

1	Egg
1 c.	Sugar
1 c.	Milk
2½ c.	Flour (sifted)
2 t.	Baking Powder
½ t.	Salt
½ c.	Chopped Pecans
1 t.	Vanilla

Mix well. Pour into floured and greased loaf pan. Bake at 325° for about 1 hour.
For Banana Nut Bread add 2 very ripe bananas that have been put through a sieve.

PECAN CREAM CHEESE SWEET ROLLS

2 pkg.	Crescent Rolls
8 oz.	Cream Cheese
¼ c.	Sugar
½ c.	Chopped Pecans
3 T.	Dark Brown Sugar
2 t.	Ground Cinnamon
¾ c.	Powdered Sugar
2 T.	Milk
1 t.	Vanilla

Soften cream cheese and add ¼ c. sugar and ½ t. vanilla. Combine pecans, brown sugar, and cinnamon. Press 2 pieces of crescent dough together to make a rectangle. Spread with cream cheese mixture, then sprinkle with pecan mixture, and roll into a log shape. Continue this process with the rest of the crescent dough. Refrigerate for at least 30 minutes until the cream cheese has hardened again. Remove and cut each roll into 4 pieces. Bake at 375° for about 15 minutes. Allow to cool. Combine powdered sugar and milk heat slowly in a sauce pan and bring to a boil. Add ½ t. vanilla and cook this down a bit. Allow this mixture to cool and then glaze the rolls with it. Yield 32.

Orange Cream Cheese Sweet Rolls

2 pkgs.	Crescent Rolls
8 oz.	Cream Cheese
6 T.	Orange Juice
2 T.	Sugar
½ c.	Powdered Sugar
2 t.	Orange Zest
1 t.	Vanilla

Soften cream cheese, then add 3T. orange juice, 2T. sugar, 1t. orange zest and ½ t. vanilla. Press 2 pieces of crescent dough together to make a rectangle. Spread cream cheese mixture over the dough and roll into a log. Continue this process with all of the dough. Refrigerate at least 30 minutes until cream cheese has hardened again. Remove and cut each rolls into 4 pieces. Bake at 375° for about 15 minutes. Allow to cool.

Combine powdered sugar, 3T. orange juice, 1t. orange zest in a sauce pan. Slowly bring to a boil, and add ½ t. vanilla. Cook down a bit. Then allow to cool.
Glaze rolls with this mixture. Yield 32.

BeBe's Brownies

2 stick	Butter (not margarine)
2 c.	Sugar
4 large	Eggs
4 squares	Melted Baker's Unsweetened Chocolate
½ c.	Flour
1 lb.	Chopped Pecans

Melt chocolate and set aside. Cream butter and sugar until it looks like cleansing cream. Add eggs one at a time and beat well after each addition. Add melted chocolate and mix well. Add flour, beating well until satiny. Add pecans. Pour into a well-greased pan. Do not use a glass baking dish. Place in preheated 350° oven for 30-40 minutes (until toothpick inserted into the center comes out clean). When done, cool slightly and press down with a dishcloth.

FROSTING:

1 stick	Butter
3 T.	Cocoa
6 T.	Coca Cola (the Real Thing, do not substitute)
1 t.	Vanilla
1 box	Powdered Sugar

Place butter, cocoa, and Coca Cola in sauce pan and bring to a boil. Remove from heat, and add vanilla and powdered sugar. Beat until glossy. Cover the brownies with frosting. Cover the pan with foil and refrigerate for several hours before cutting.

Brownies must be kept in refrigerator, tightly covered.

BeBe is our friend who used to live in the condos in Florida where my family has a place. She is from Oklahoma, and is quite a character.

Cookies & Candy

Cookies & Candy

OATMEAL COOKIES

1 c.	Crisco
1 c.	Sugar
1 c.	Dark Brown Sugar (packed)
2	Eggs
2 T.	Water
1½ c.	Flour
1 t.	Baking Soda
1 t.	Salt
3 c.	Oatmeal
1 t.	Vanilla
1½ c.	Milk Chocolate Chips or Raisins
1½ c.	Chopped Pecans

Cream Crisco and sugar. Add eggs, and then the rest of the ingredients. Mix well. Spoon onto a lightly greased cookie sheet and bake at 375° for 8-10 minutes. Yield: 5-6 dozen.

Sometimes we will separate the dough before adding the chips or raisins, and make half with the chocolate chips and half with the raisins.

Oatmeal Cookies

CRESCENTS

½ lb.	Butter
5T. (heaping)	Powdered Sugar
2 c.	Flour
½ c.	Pecans
1 t.	Vanilla
	Pinch of Salt

Cream butter and sugar. Add flour, a small amount at a time. Add other ingredients and mix well. Pinch off in small pieces and shape into crescents. Place on a cookie sheet and bake in a slow oven (300°-325°) for 15-20 minutes. Allow to cool, and roll in powdered sugar. Yield: 7-8 dozen.

ICE BOX COOKIES

6 c.	Sifted Flour
1 box	Dark Brown Sugar
1 lb.	Margarine or Butter
1	Egg
1 t.	Baking Powder
1 c.	Chopped Pecans
1 t.	Vanilla

Mix well. Roll into 1" diameter by 12-14" cylinders. Freeze well, and cut into cookies. Bake at 350°-375° until brown – about 10 minutes. Yield: 8-10 dozen.

JEANNE'S LEMON SQUARES

CRUST:
½ c.	Butter
1 c.	Flour
¼ c.	Powdered Sugar

Mix and press in a 9"x9" pan. Bake at 350° for 15 minutes.

FILLING:
2	Eggs (beaten)
2 T.	Flour
1 c.	Sugar
½ t.	Baking Powder
2 T.	Lemon Juice and Rind

Mix well. Pour over crust. Bake at 350° for 20 minutes. Sprinkle with powdered sugar and lemon juice. Cut into squares.

From our deceased friend Jeanne Allen, who we all miss.

FUDGE CANDY

2 c.	Sugar
4 T.	Cocoa
1 c.	Half and Half Cream
2 T.	Butter
¾ c.	Chopped pecans
1 t.	Vanilla

Mix sugar and cocoa, add milk, cook until a soft ball can be formed when tested in cold water. Remove from heat, add butter and vanilla. Let cool and beat about 15 minutes, or until creamy. Add nuts. Pour into buttered dish. Let set and cut into squares.

Fudge Candy

CARAMEL CANDY

3 c.	Sugar
1 c.	Milk
1 c.	Sugar – browned in iron skillet
1 t.	Vanilla
1 T.	Butter
1 c.	Chopped pecans

Cook 3 c. sugar in milk until it forms a soft ball in cold water. Add browned sugar and boil 1 minute. Add butter and vanilla. Beat until it thickens. Add nuts, and drop in spoonfuls on waxed paper.

SUGARED WALNUTS (PECANS) #1

2 ½ c.	Nuts (halves)
1 c.	Sugar
½ c.	Water
1 t.	Maple Flavoring
½ t.	Salt
½ t.	Vanilla

Toast nuts at 375° for 10 minutes. Cool. Mix sugar, flavoring, salt and water in a saucepan. Stir until sugar dissolves. Cook uncovered to 230° or soft ball. Add vanilla and nuts. Stir until nuts are well covered and sugar is crystallized. Pour out on a board and separate as they cool.

SUGARED PECANS #2

1 lb.	Pecan Halves
1½ stick	Butter
2	Egg Whites (beaten)
1 c.	Sugar
1 t.	Cinnamon
1 t.	Vanilla

Mix beaten egg whites, sugar and cinnamon. Melt butter and pour into mixture. Fold in nuts and vanilla. Spread on an ungreased cookie sheet. Bake at 325° for about 30 minutes. Stir every 10 minutes. When done they shouldn't look wet, but shine.

Pies & Desserts

Pies & Desserts

SKILLET CHOCOLATE PIE

1 c.	Sugar
4 T.	Flour
3 T.	Cocoa
3	Egg Yolks
1½ c.	Milk
1½ T.	Butter
1 t.	Vanilla

MERINGUE:

3	Egg Whites
6 T.	Sugar
½ t.	Vanilla

Mix dry ingredients in an iron skillet. Beat egg yolks. Add egg yolks and milk to dry ingredients Cook over low to medium heat, stirring constantly until thick. Add butter and vanilla. Pour into partially baked pie crust and bake about 10 minutes at 400°. Beat egg whites and sugar until stiff, add vanilla. Spread over the top of chocolate mixture. Bake at 300° for 15-20 minutes.

BOBBY'S FUDGE PIE

1 stick	Butter
2 squares	Baking Chocolate*
1 c.	Sugar
2	Eggs
¼ c.	Flour
1 t.	Salt
1 t.	Vanilla

Melt chocolate. Remove from heat and cool. Stir in sugar, add 2 beaten eggs and flour. Add salt and vanilla. Pour into greased and floured aluminum pie pan. Bake at 400° for 25 minutes.

*Bobby uses 1 semi-sweet square and 1 unsweetened square. When he doubles the recipe, he adds an extra square of semi-sweet.

I really think that Bobby got this from his mother, Barbara, who was Mama's best friend.

Bobby and Pam Chilton and Susan

CHESS PIE

3	Eggs (beaten)
1½ c.	Sugar
1 stick	Butter
1 T.	Vanilla
1 t.	Vinegar

Cream sugar and butter. Add eggs, vanilla, and vinegar. Pour into unbaked pie shell, and bake for 1 hour at 325°. If using tart shells, this will make 12-14, and don't bake as long.

Chess pie originated (according to legend) at Belle Meade Plantation. It was "just pie", but came to be pronounced "chess pie".

CHOCOLATE CHESS PIE

2 c.	Sugar
1 stick	Butter
3	Eggs
1 T.	Flour
1 T. (heaping)	Cocoa
1 t.	Vanilla
1 small can	Pet Evaporated Milk

Cream butter and sugar. Add well beaten eggs, cocoa, flour, milk, and vanilla. Beat, beat, beat with a hand mixer. Pour into 2 uncooked pie shells. Bake at 375° for 25-30 minutes. If using tarts, this will make 26-30. Don't bake them as long.

Chess Pie

GRASSHOPPER PIE

CRUST:

20	Oreos (crushed)
½ c.	Melted Butter

FILLING:

30	Marshmallows
1 c.	Powdered Sugar
3 T.	Cream de Menthe
3 T.	White Crème de Cocoa
½ c.	Milk

Place milk and marshmallows in a double boiler. When marshmallows are melted, add other ingredients. Cook until well mixed. Pour into 2 pie crusts, and put in freezer until frozen.

Pecan Pie

½ c.	Light Karo Syrup
½ c.	Sugar
2	Eggs
1 T.	Butter
½ c.	Pecans
1 t.	Vanilla
	Pinch of Salt

Bake pie crust for 10 minutes at 375°. Mix ingredients and pour into pie shell. Bake for 30 minutes at 325°.

EASIEST COBBLER EVER

1 stick	Butter
½ c.	Flour
½ c.	Sugar
1 t. (heaping)	Baking Powder
½ t.	Salt
½ c.	Milk
2-2 ½ c.	Fruit (mix with ¼ to ½ c. sugar)

Melt butter in 1 quart baking dish. Mix flour, sugar, baking powder and salt. Add milk and stir thoroughly. Pour into dish with butter, but do not stir. Cut up fruit and stir in additional sugar. Pour this into the dish, but do not stir. Bake at 350° for 20-30 minutes until top is golden brown.

I have used blackberries, peaches, and blueberries for this. You can use canned fruit like cherries as well (be sure to drain them). Some fruits are sweeter than others, and will need to have a little more sugar added.

This is an easy recipe to double.

CHOCOLATE HEATH TORTE ("STUFF")

36 single	Macaroons
1 qt.	Chocolate Ice Cream
1 qt.	Vanilla or Coffee Ice Cream
6 T.	Chocolate Sauce (page 170)
5	Heath Bars (crumbled)

Oil an oblong pan or casserole (9 x13). Crush 18 macaroons and spread in the bottom of the pan. Spread softened chocolate ice cream over the top, then drizzle 3 T. of the chocolate sauce over this. Crush 18 more macaroons and spread on top, and then spread with softened vanilla ice cream. Drizzle the remaining 3 T. of chocolate sauce over this, and then sprinkle crumbled Heath bars over the top. Freeze again before serving.

We call this "Stuff". It is sooo good.
I make macaroons according to the recipe on the Solo Almond Paste can, but you can buy them.

Meringue Kisses

6   **Eggs Whites**
12 T.   **Sugar**
1 t.   **Vanilla**

Beat eggs whites and sugar until stiff. Add vanilla. Drop on a cookie sheet that has been covered with brown paper. Bake in a low oven 200 – 225 for 1 hour.
Do not allow to brown.

If using these for ice cream, after dropping on the cookie sheet, make an indentation with a spoon.

To make cookies, add pecans and or chocolate chips (about 1/2 c. of each).

COVERED CHERRIES

1 stick	Butter (melted)
1½ c.	Powdered Sugar
¾ c.	Coconut (flaked)
¾ c.	Macaroons (crumbled)
1 T.	Evaporated Milk
½ t.	Almond Extract
1½-2 c.	Graham Cracker Crumbs
1 jar	Maraschino Cherries (with stems)

Mix all ingredients except cherries and graham cracker crumbs. Drain cherries on a paper towel. Cover cherries with mixture, and then roll in graham cracker crumbs. Refrigerate. This will make a good many, so use a pretty large size jar of cherries.

BANANA PUDDING

4-5 large	Bananas
1 2/3c. + 8 T.	Sugar
1½ c.	Milk or Cream
3 T.	Flour (heaping)
1 t.	Vanilla
4	Eggs
	Vanilla Wafers

Separate eggs. In a double boiler, beat yolks. Add 1 2/3 c. sugar with flour. Add milk and cook, stirring constantly until it thickens. Add vanilla. In a deep baking dish, place a layer of wafers. Cover with bananas, and pour some of the custard. Make 1-2 more layers. Beat egg whites with 8 T. sugar until stiff. Cover pudding, and run under the broiler until brown. Serves 10-12.

My great aunt "Bibbie" taught me how to make her banana pudding.

CHOCOLATE ÉCLAIRS

PASTRY:

6 T.	Butter
¾ c.	Sifted Flour
¾ c.	Water
3	Eggs

In a saucepan bring butter and water to a boil. Reduce heat and rapidly stir in flour. Cook and stir until mixture leaves the side of the pan. Remove from heat and beat in eggs one at a time until mixture is satiny. On a cookie sheet, form strips of dough a little over 1" long. Bake at 425° for 10 minutes. (If you want to make larger éclairs, make longer, wider strips, and cook longer.) Then cook at 350° for 15-20 minutes until the tops are brown.

FILLING:

1 c.	Whipping Cream
1 box	Vanilla Pudding

Mix well. Cut tops off of éclairs, and put a small spoon of filling in each. Place top back on and frost.

FROSTING:

1 stick	Butter
6 T.	Evaporated Milk
1 box	Powdered Sugar
3 T.	Cocoa
1 t.	Vanilla
	A small bit of egg white

Beat this mixture until it is thick, and frost the éclairs.
Refrigerate. Make 40-50 small éclairs.

LEMON SOUFFLÉ

1 – 1½ c.	Vanilla Wafer Crumbs
6	Eggs (separated)
1¼ c.	Sugar
½ c.	Fresh Squeezed Lemon Juice
1 c.	Whipping Cream

Cover the bottom of a soufflé or trifle dish with all but a couple of tablespoons of the wafer crumbs. Beat egg whites until stiff adding sugar gradually. Add egg yolks 1 at a time, beating well after each. Add lemon juice and mix well. Whip cream and fold into the mixture. Turn into crumb lined dish. Top with wafer crumbs. Freeze. Before serving, garnish with thin slices of lemon. Serves 10-12.

NOTE: This recipe contains uncooked eggs.

TIRAMISU

6	Egg Yolks
1¼ c.	Sugar
1¼ c.	Mascarpone Cheese
1¾ c.	Whipped Cream
1 t.	Vanilla
2 – 3oz. pkg.	Lady Fingers
½ c.	Coffee Liqueur or Brandied Espresso
1 c.	Sweetened Whipped Cream
	Cocoa
	Curled Chocolate Pieces

In a double boiler, combine egg yolks and sugar. Whip until thick and lemon colored – about 1 minute. Place over boiling water. Reduce heat to low and cook 8-10 minutes, stirring constantly. Add mascarpone cheese, vanilla, and beat well. Remove from heat Whip cream until stiff. Fold cream into egg mixture and set aside. Line the bottom of a 3-qt. bowl or trifle dish with ladyfingers. Drizzle with coffee liqueur (or espresso). Spoon on half of egg-cream mixture. Repeat layer. Top with sweetened whipped cream, and sprinkle with cocoa and garnish with chocolate curls. Cover and refrigerate several hours or overnight. Serves 10-12.

BRANDIED ESPRESSO:

½ c.	Water
3 t.	Instant Coffee
2 T.	Brandy

Combine boiling water with coffee, and stir until granules are dissolved. Add brandy, and allow to cool.

SWEETENED WHIPPED CREAM:

1 c.	Whipping Cream
3 T.	Sugar
½ t.	Vanilla

Combine cream and sugar, and whipped until stiff peaks form. Add vanilla and mix well.

TRIFLE

4 c.	Boiled Custard (see: Beverages)
8 oz.	Lady Fingers
8 oz.	Macaroons (broken)
5 T.	Sherry
1 pt. jar	Red Raspberry Preserves
1 c.	Whipping Cream
½ c.	Blanched Almonds (chopped)

In a trifle bowl, layer lady fingers and macaroons. Drizzle with sherry. Top with raspberry preserves, then custard. Make at least one more layer. Spread whipped cream over the top and sprinkle on almonds. Refrigerate. Serves 10-12.

FLAN

1 pt.	Whipping Cream
4	Egg Yolks
½ c.	Sugar
1 t.	Vanilla

TOPPING:
1 T.	Sugar
2 t.	Dark Brown Sugar

Preheat oven to 350°. Heat cream on stove until it bubbles around the edges. Don't boil. Beat egg yolks and sugar with an electric mixer until thick, gradually beating in hot cream. Add vanilla. Pour into 4-6 ramekins and place in ½ inch water bath. Bake until they set – about 25 minutes. Combine sugars and sprinkle on top. Put on the top rack of oven and broil until sugar melts. Chill.

APRICOT FRIED PIES

2 pkg.	Dried Apricots
1 c.	Sugar
	Water
	Prepared Pie Pastry

Gently boil apricots in water and sugar until they become almost like preserves. Add more sugar if needed. Roll pastry out until it's pretty thin. Cut rounds with largest biscuit cutter. Place a spoonful of apricots on a round and fold over. Crimp with a fork around the edges. Fry in a skillet with a small amount of oil until browned on both sides. If you don't want to fry them, bake in a 350° oven until browned on both sides.

Peaches or apples can be used instead of apricots.

ALMOND ICE BOX PIE

6	Egg yolks
1 box	Powdered Sugar
1 t.	Vanilla
1 t.	Almond flavoring
1 c.	Chopped almonds
	Graham cracker crumbs

Beat egg yolks well and add sugar. Continue beating, add flavoring and almonds. Cover the bottom of an oblong 2 qt. Pyrex with graham cracker crumbs. Press mixture on top of crumbs and sprinkle crumbs on top. Store in refrigerator or freezer until ready to serve. Cut in squares and top with vanilla ice cream. Serves 12-15.

NOTE: This recipe contains uncooked eggs.

Beverages

FRUIT TEA

10-12	Tea Bags
1 sm. can	Frozen Orange Juice
1 sm. can	Frozen Lemonade
1 c.	Sugar

Dissolve sugar in boiling water and allow to cool. Steep tea bags in boiling water and allow to cool. In a 1 gallon pitcher or jar, pour sugar water, tea, orange juice and lemonade. Add water until you have a gallon. Mix well and chill before serving.

Fruit tea is great in the spring and summer especially. My family drinks it year round. It must be a concoction indigenous to our area, because when we serve it to people from other states, they seem to have never had it before.

Susan and Shauna Palk toast to tailgating.

Instant Hot Tea Mix

½ c.   **Instant Tea**

2 c.   **Tang**

Lemonade Mix (Country Time)
Use the amount of mix that makes 2 Qt.

2 c.   **Sugar**

2 t.   **Ground Cinnamon**

2 t.   **Ground Clove**

Mix in a bowl, and then spoon into jars. Use 2 t. to a cup of boiling water. Keeps indefinitely.

I have put this into fancy jars, and given it away at Christmas.

PARTY PUNCH

2 c.	Coconut rum
2 c.	Mango juice
2 c.	Pineapple-Orange juice

Mix together and chill. Add white rum if desired for more of a kick.

Our friends Mark and Damon gave us this. It's great to serve around the pool on a hot day.

24 HOUR COCKTAIL

1 dz.	Lemons
1 dz.	Oranges
1 qt.	Whiskey
1 c.	Sugar

Grind lemons and oranges. Put all ingredients in a jar and let stand 24 hours. Strain and bottle. The longer it is kept, the better.

I found this in my grandmother's recipes and just had to add it for fun. Personally I have never tried it, so proceed at your own risk.

BOILED CUSTARD

2 or 3	Eggs
1 T.	Flour
1 c.	Sugar
1 qt.	Scalded Milk or Cream
1 t.	Vanilla

Scald milk. Mix beaten eggs, sugar and flour. Pour into heated milk. Stir constantly until it thickens, then add vanilla. Strain and refrigerate. When ready to serve, top with whipped cream and "flavor" with bourbon. This is a single recipe, it should always be doubled at least.

This is a holiday favorite around our house. K.K. has become an expert at making boiled custard.

Prep Work

Prep Work

Preparation is most important, especially when working on a dinner party or other type of entertainment event. If you are not organized, it can become chaotic when trying to get it together.

Start by making lists. First, list the menu. After this, look up all the recipes you are using, and take stock of what you need from the grocery. Be sure to check everything. Just because you think you have enough flour, it is not a certainty. Decide what other items you'll need – liquor, paper products, candles, etc. Then finally, make a list of the order in which you'll prepare the meal.

Try to do all of your shopping at once – usually a couple of days before the event. This is sometimes not possible. When using fresh vegetables or fruit, you don't want them sitting around too long.

You'll probably be able to fix at least some of the items a day in advance. The more you can do ahead of time, the better. Just be sure you have enough room to store everything.

One thing that I can't stress enough is to always start with a clean kitchen. Whether you tidy up when you end the day, or start the next, be sure things are in order. I have a very small kitchen, and when it's not clean, it's a mess and can completely throw me off.

Finally, don't panic in the end. Decide what needs to come out and when, and ahead of time, have a place on the table planned for each dish.

Menus

Luncheon 1

...ato Aspic with Chicken Salad
Cheese Soufflé
Asparagus Roll-ups
Ella's Rolls with Ham
Chocolate Chess Tarts

Luncheon 2

Assorted Sandwiches - quartered
Chicken Salad
Pimento Cheese
...m Cheese Olive Nut
Pasta Salad
...ford's Vegetable Salad
...hocolate Chip Cookies

Luncheon 3

Jea...
Oat...
Shrimp D... over Shredded Lettuce
Garnis... Quartered Tomatoes
Qua... Hardboiled Eggs
...ed Avocado
...se Dreams
...n Soufflé

Menus

Here are some menus that combine different dishes to make a meal. In most cases, these are combinations that we use. It might help when planning for different occasions, but I'm sure you can come up with your own.

BRUNCH 1

Egg, Sausage, and Brie Casserole
Cheese Grits
Fresh Fruit with Poppy Seed Dressing
Sour Cream Coffee Cake
Ella's Rolls

BRUNCH 2

Quiche
Potato Casserole
Baked Apples
Banana Nut Muffins
Biscuits

BRUNCH 3

Shrimp and Grits
Eggs Vermicelli
Frozen Fruit Salad
Pecan Cream Cheese Sweet Rolls
Orange Cream Cheese Sweet Rolls
Potato Rolls

LUNCHEON 1

Tomato Aspic with Chicken Salad
Cheese Soufflé
Asparagus Roll-ups
Ella's Rolls with Ham
Chocolate Chess Tarts

LUNCHEON 2

Assorted Sandwiches – quartered
Chicken Salad
Pimento Cheese
Cream Cheese Olive Nut

Pasta Salad
Jean Crawford's Vegetable Salad
Oatmeal Chocolate Chip Cookies

LUNCHEON 3

Shrimp Delight over Shredded Lettuce
Garnishes: Quartered Tomatoes
Quartered Hardboiled Eggs
Sliced Avocado

Cheese Dreams
Lemon Soufflé

LUNCHEON 4

Chicken Artichoke Soup
Tossed Salad with Sesame Dressing
Bread Sticks
Fudge Pie

Summer Luncheon

Chicken Salad with Fresh Tomatoes
Fresh Fruit with Poppy Seed Dressing
Cheese Soufflé
Ham and Rolls
Crescents
Ice Box Cookies

Sunday Dinner 1

Fried Chicken
Fresh Lima Beans
Squash Casserole
Fried Corn
Cornbread
Chicken Gravy
Blackberry Cobbler

Sunday Dinner 2

Pork Roast
Turnip Greens
Candied Sweet Potatoes
Slaw
Corn Bread Cakes
Chess Pie

Sunday Dinner 3

Pull Apart (Pot Roast) with Carrots and Potatoes
Green Beans
Squash Casserole
Spoon Bread
Skillet Chocolate Pie

Sunday Dinner 4

Meat Loaf
Mashed Potatoes
Cabbage
Black Eyed Peas
Fried Green Tomatoes
Corn Light Bread
Buttermilk Cake with Ice Cream and Chocolate Sauce

Cocktail Buffet 1

Beef Tenderloin with Horseradish Sauce
Ella's Rolls
Chicken Salad in Pastry Shells
Shrimp Mold with Crackers
Date Nut Bread with Cream Cheese
Hot Artichoke Dip
Vegetable Tray with Vegetable Dip
Crab Toasts
Dessert Tray: Fudge Cake
Chess Cake
Crescents

Cocktail Buffet 2

Pork Tenderloin with Honey Mustard Sauce
Rolls
Smoked Salmon on Baguette
Cheese Tray: Baked Brie en Croute
Pineapple Cheese Ball
Wedge of Bleu Cheese
Cubed Gouda
Strawberries & Grapes
Crackers
Broccoli Dip with Fritos
Tomato and Cucumber Sandwiches
Spinach Squares
Dessert Tray: Individual Cheese Cakes
Chocolate Éclairs

SUPPER 1

Chicken Artichoke Casserole
Rice
Salad with Sesame Dressing
Bread
Chocolate Heath Torte

SUPPER 2

Lasagna
Spinach Salad with Dressing
Bread
Tiramisu

SUPPER 3

Beef Tenderloin with Horseradish Sauce
Twice Baked Potatoes
Fresh Asparagus with Hollandaise Sauce
Congealed Cranberry Salad
Ella's Rolls
Almond Ice Box Pie with Vanilla Ice Cream

SUPPER 4

Fried Fish and Shrimp
Potato Casserole
Ramen Noodle Slaw
Sliced Tomatoes
Hush Puppies (use mix and add onion)
Ellen's Rum Cake

SUPPER 5

Tarragon Pork Chops
Risotto Parmesan
Green Bean Casserole
Baked Tomatoes
Spoon Bread
Banana Pudding

WINTER SUPPER

Mama's Vegetable Soup
Layered Salad
Hot Water Corn Cakes
Skillet Chocolate Pie

TAILGATE MEAL

Chili
Empanadas
Nine Layered Dip
Mary's Mango Salsa
Variety of Chips
Mexican Corn Bread
Oatmeal Cookies

LATE NIGHT SUPPER

Omelet
Fresh Fruit with Bobby's Quick Dressing
Crab Toasts

Thanksgiving/Christmas Dinner

Turkey
Cornbread Dressing
Mashed Potatoes
Mashed Sweet Potatoes
Fresh Lima Beans
Asparagus Casserole
Deviled Oysters
Congealed Cranberry Salad
Ella's Rolls
Yellow Cake with Caramel Icing
Coconut Cake
Boiled Custard

Easter Dinner

Grilled Lamb
Rice Casserole
Candied Sweet Potatoes
Fresh Asparagus with Hollandaise Sauce
Fresh Lima Beans
Congealed Cranberry Salad
Rolls
Meringue Kisses with Ice Cream and Fresh Strawberries

Entertainment Journal

DATE:_____

OCCASION:_____

GUESTS:

_____   _____

_____   _____

_____   _____

_____   _____

_____   _____

_____   _____

MENU:

_____   _____

_____   _____

_____   _____

_____   _____

_____   _____

DATE:_____

OCCASION:_____

GUESTS:

_____   _____

_____   _____

_____   _____

_____   _____

_____   _____

_____   _____

_____   _____

MENU:

_____   _____

_____   _____

_____   _____

_____   _____

_____   _____

DATE:_____

OCCASION:_____

GUESTS:

_____   _____

_____   _____

_____   _____

_____   _____

_____   _____

_____   _____

_____   _____

MENU:

_____   _____

_____   _____

_____   _____

_____   _____

_____   _____

_____   _____

DATE:_____

OCCASION:_____

GUESTS:

_____   _____

_____   _____

_____   _____

_____   _____

_____   _____

_____   _____

_____   _____

MENU:

_____   _____

_____   _____

_____   _____

_____   _____

_____   _____

_____   _____

DATE:_____

OCCASION:_____

GUESTS:

_____   _____

_____   _____

_____   _____

_____   _____

_____   _____

_____   _____

_____   _____

MENU:

_____   _____

_____   _____

_____   _____

_____   _____

_____   _____

_____   _____

DATE:_____

OCCASION:_____

GUESTS:

_____   _____

_____   _____

_____   _____

_____   _____

_____   _____

_____   _____

_____   _____

MENU:

_____   _____

_____   _____

_____   _____

_____   _____

_____   _____

_____   _____

DATE:_____

OCCASION:_____

GUESTS:

_____ _____

_____ _____

_____ _____

_____ _____

_____ _____

_____ _____

_____ _____

MENU:

_____ _____

_____ _____

_____ _____

_____ _____

_____ _____

_____ _____

Susan & Mama

l. to r. - Mama, Susan, Polly (Cullen),
Ellen (Mayo), Neill (Pitts)
and K.K. (Rainey)

Family Favorites

Susan and her son, Perry

l. to r. - Susan, Jenny (Pappas) Breeden,
Laura (Massey) Bearden,
Rebecca (Ozborn) Marshall,
Judy Traughber, and Linda (Martin) Miller.

Family Favorites

RECIPE	PAGE NUMBER

RECIPE

PAGE NUMBER

RECIPE

PAGE NUMBER

_____

_____

_____

_____

_____

_____

_____

_____

_____

_____

_____

_____

_____

_____

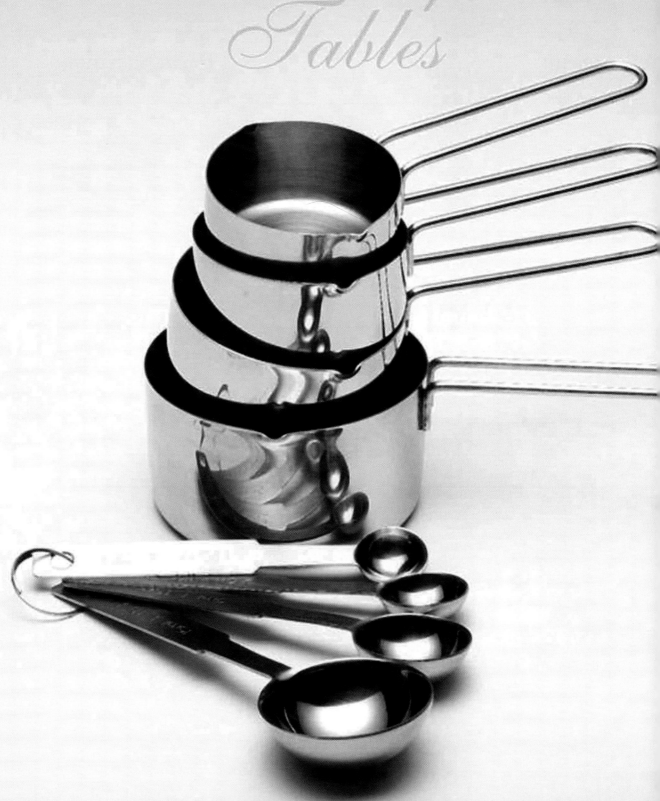

Measurement/Equivalent Tables

Measurement/Equivalent Tables

TABLE OF MEASUREMENTS

Speck, dash, few grains (dry)	Less than 1/8 teaspoon
Dash (liquid)	A few drops
3 teaspoons	1 tablespoon
½ of 1 tablespoon	1 ½ teaspoon
2 tablespoons	1/8 cup
2 tablespoons	1 liquid once
4 tablespoons	¼ cup
5 tablespoons + 1 teaspoon	1/3 cup
8 tablespoons	½ cup
12 tablespoons	¾ cup
16 tablespoons	1 cup
1 cup	½ pint (liquid)
2 cups (16 fluid oz.)	1 pint
4 cups	1 quart
2 pints	1 quart
4 quarts	1 gallon
8 quarts	1 peck
4 pecks	1 bushel
16 ounces	1 pound
1 jigger	1 ½ fluid oz. (3 tablespoons)
1 large jigger	2 fluid oz. (1/4 cup)

LIQUID MEASUREMENTS
(to the nearest equivalents)

Cups/Spoons:	Quarts/Ounces:	Metric Equivalents:
1 teaspoon	1/6 ounce	5 milliliters/5 grams
2 teaspoons	1/3 ounce	10 milliliters/10 grams
1 tablespoon	½ ounce	15 milliliters/15 grams
3 1/3 tablespoons	1 ¾ ounces	50 milliliters
¼ cup (4 tablespoons)	2 ounces	60 milliliters
1/3 cup(5 1/3 tablespoons)	2 2/3 ounces	79 milliliters
1/3 cup + 1 tablespoon	3 ½ ounces	100 milliliters
½ cup (8 tablespoons)	4 ounces	118 milliliters
1 cup (16 tablespoons)	8 ounces	¼ liter/236 milliliters
2 cups	1 pint/16 ounces	½ liter -1½ tablespoons
2 cups + 2 ½ tablespoons	17 ounces	½ liter
4 cups	1 quart/32 ounces	946 milliliters
4 1/3 cups	1 quart, 2 ounces	1 liter/1000 milliliters

OVEN HEATS

250 degrees – Very slow	350 degrees – Moderate
300 degrees – Slow	375 degrees – Moderately Hot
325 degrees – Moderately slow	450 –500 degrees – Very hot

TEMPERATURE DEFINITIONS

180 degrees - Simmering point of water

212 degrees – Boiling point of water

234-240 degrees – Soft ball stage for syrups

255 degrees – Hard crack stage for syrups

320 degrees – Caramel stage for syrups

220 degrees – Jellying point for jams and jellies

At altitudes above 3000 feet, lower air pressure causes differences in the boiling point of water and syrups.

TABLE OF EQUIVALENTS

Almonds, chopped	4 ½ c	3 ½ lbs., unshelled
Apples	3 lbs.	about 2 qt., sliced
Asparagus	20 stalks	1lb.
Baking Powder	1 teaspoon	1/3 t. baking soda + ½ t. cream of tartar
Bananas, skins on	3 large	1lb.
Beans, fresh green	1 qt.	3¼ lb.
Beans, dried	1 c.	½ lb.
Bread Crumbs	1 c.	2¾ oz.
Butter	2c.	1lb.
Butter	1 stick	½ c.
Cheese, grated	1lb.	4c.
Cheese, cottage	1lb.	2c.
Cheese, cream	6T.	3 oz.
Chocolate, unsweetened	1 square	1 oz.
Corn Meal	3c.	1lb.
Cornstarch	1T.	2T. flour
Crab Meat	2c.	1 lb.
Crackers, graham	3c., crumbs	30-36 crackers
Crackers, salted	1c., fine crumbs	20 crackers
Dates, pitted	2c.	1lb.
Eggs:		
Whole	1 egg	about 3T.
	5-6 eggs	1c.
Whites	1 white	about 2T.
	8-10 whites	1 c.
Yolks	1 yolk	about 1T.
	14-16 yolks	1c.
Flour, unsifted	3c.	1lb.
All-purpose, shifted	3 ¾ c.	1lb.
Cake, sifted	2c.	1lb.

TABLE OF EQUIVALENTS (CONT.)

Gelatin, unflavored	1 envelope	1T.
Lemon	1 medium	2-3T.
Macaroni	1-1½c. dry (4oz.)	2¼c., cooked
Marshmallows	30 standard size	½ pound
	1 standard size	10 miniatures
Noodles	1½-2c. dry (4oz.)	2¼ c., cooked
Nuts, chopped	4c.	1lb.
Orange, juiced	1	6-8T.
Pecans, chopped	3c.	1 lb.
Punch	1 gallon	serves approx. 20
	12 quarts	96 punch cups
Raisins, seedless	3c.	1lb.
Rice	1c. raw	3-3½ c., cooked
	1c.	½ lb.
Shrimp, cooked	2c.	1lb.
Sugar:		
Granulated	1c.	½ lb.
Confectioners	3½ c.	1lb.
Brown	2½ c., firmly packed	1lb.
Tomatoes	4	1lb.
Walnuts, English	4c., chopped	2½ lb., unshelled
Water	1c.	½ lb.
Yeast	1 cake	1 level T. dry
Vanilla Wafers	1c., crumbs	about 22 wafers

Kitchen Hints

✓ Fruits and vegetables ripen faster when they are placed in a paper bag or newspaper, and stored in a drawer or closed cupboard.

✓ Use the drying cycle of the dish washer for a heat drawer.

✓ To crisp limp celery, place it in a pan of cold water and add a slice of raw potato. Let it stand for a few hours.

✓ To mince parsley easier, bunch the leafy tops together, and cut with scissors into a measuring cup. Then to mince finer, put the scissors in the cup, and chop away.

✓ To keep parsley fresh for up to three weeks, place in a dry, screw-top bottle and refrigerate.

✓ Put a dry sponge in the vegetable drawer of the refrigerator to absorb moisture.

✓ To keep ready-to-use whipped cream on hand, whip 1 pint of cream with 4T. sugar. Drop in peaks on a cookie sheet and freeze. Transfer them to an airtight container, and store in the freezer. Remove 15 minutes before serving.

✓ To keep rolls or toast hot longer, put a piece of foil under the napkin in the serving basket.

✓ To reheat rolls, place them in a wet brown paper bag, and then in the oven.

✓ To peel hard boiled eggs easier, put salt in the water when cooking them, and then plunge them in to cold water after removing them from the heat. Eggs that are not so fresh always peel better.

✓ Egg yolks will keep up to three days, if they are covered in cold water and then refrigerated.

✓ Allow egg whites to warm up to room temperature before beating them.

✓ To make salad dressing have a fuller flavor, mix any seasonings with the vinegar before adding the oil. Oil coats herbs and traps the flavor.

✓ To keep cookies crisper, put a crushed piece of tissue paper in the bottom of the cookie jar.

✓ Unshelled nuts keep indefinitely in the freezer.

✓ To cut meringue pies easier, sprinkle a little sugar over the meringue before browning it.

✓ Scrambled eggs will be fluffier if a little carbonated water is added.

✓ Use an egg slicer to slice raw mushrooms evenly and quickly.

✓ To cut fresh bread, heat the serrated knife first.

✓ Cheese can be sliced thinner if a dull knife is used.

✓ To keep an avocado that has been cut from turning brown, refrigerate it with its seed until ready to serve.

✓ To eliminate unpleasant cooking odors, simmer some vinegar on the stove.

✓ To keep cakes fresh, put a half of an apple in the container.

✓ To flour chicken for frying, place it in a paper bag and shake. Cookies can be covered with powdered sugar the same way.

✓ To measure molasses or syrups, grease the cup in which it is being measured to make it easier to pour.

✓ Sprinkle salt in a frying pan before frying meat to prevent the fat from splashing.

✓ Peel an onion under water to keep the tears back.

✓ To freshen wilted greens, douse them quickly in hot water, then ice water with a little vinegar added.

✓ To blanch almonds, cover the shelled almonds with boiling water, allow them to cool, and slip the skins off.

✓ Wrap a cloth moistened with vinegar around cheese to keep it fresh.

✓ To keep noodles from boiling over, add a tablespoon of butter to the water.

✓ Dip citrus fruit into boiling water before squeezing to increase the amount of juice.

✓ A pinch of salt added to sugar in icings will prevent it from graining.

Index

Index

A

Almond Cake with Raspberry Sauce 214
Almond Ice Box Pie 255
APPETIZERS
    Bacon Wrapped Water Chestnuts or Shrimp 19
    Baked Brie en Croute 5
    Bar-b-que Smokies 26
    Bread Sticks 27
    Broccoli Dip 15
    Catharine's Mini BLT's 17
    Cheese Straws 4
    Cold Artichoke Dip 9
    Cream Cheese Rolls 14
    Cucumber Ball 11
    Dip for Vegetables 28
    Ellen's Cheese Spread 18
    Empanadas 25
    Hot Artichoke Dip 8
    K.K's Spinach Dip 12
    Layered Nacho Dip 26
    Miss Polly's Crab Toasts 20
    Mozzarella Spread 29
    Pam's Spinach Squares 10
    Pineapple Cheese Ball 6
    Salmon on Baguette 21
    Sausage Pinwheels 21
    Seasoned Oyster Crackers 27
    Shrimp Mold 22
    Shrimp or Crab Puffs 23
    West Indies Salad 16
APPLES
    Baked Apples 114
APRICOT
    Apricot Fried Pies 254
    Apricot-Lemon Cake 219
ARTICHOKES
    Chicken Artichoke Casserole 148
    Chicken Artichoke Soup 44
    Cold Artichoke Spread 9
    Hot Artichoke Dip 8
ASPARAGUS
    Asparagus (Fresh) 100
    Asparagus Casserole.....101
    Hot or Cold Asparagus Roll-ups 34

B

Bacon Wrapped Water Chestnuts or Shrimp 19
Baked Apples 114
Baked Beans 120
Baked Brie en Croute 5
Baked Chicken and Rice 144
Baked Chicken Salad 146
Baked Ham 165
Baked Onion Casserole 123
Baked Tomatoes 114
Banana Muffins 217
Banana Pudding 249
Bar-b-que Smokies 26
BEANS
    Fresh Limas 106
    Green Bean Casserole 98
    Green Beans 99
BeBe's Brownies 225
Becky's Pimento Cheese Sandwiches 37
BEEF
    Beef Tenderloin 156
    Chili 49
    Country Fried Steak 158
    Empanadas 25
    Eye of Round Roast 158
    Meat Loaf 161
    Meat Sauce for Spaghetti or Lasagna 162
    Old Time Beef Hash 160
    Pull Apart (Pot Roast) 159
Bell Pepper Jelly 186
Betty B's Fettuccine 92
Betty's Caramel Icing 212
Betty's Pimento Cheese 38
BEVERAGES
    Boiled Custard 262
    Fruit Tea 258
    Instant Hot Tea Mix 260
    Party Punch 261
    24 Hour Cocktail 261
Big C's Gazpacho 43
Bleu Cheese Dressing 76
Bobby's Fudge Pie 239
Bobby's Quick and Easy Dressing for Fruit 74
Boiled Custard 262
Boiled Shrimp 131
BREADS
    Banana Muffins 217
    Bread 200
    Bread Sticks 27
    Corn Light Bread 202
    Cornbread 192
    Cornbread Cakes 196
    Cornbread Dressing 194
    Date Nut Bread 203
    Ella's Rolls 197
    Hot Water Cornbread 196
    Mexican Cornbread 201
    Nut Bread 222
    Potato Rolls 199
    Rolls 198
    Sour Cream Muffins 216
    Spoon Bread 193
Brie Sausage Egg Casserole 88
BROCCOLI
    Broccoli Dip 15
    Broccoli Ring 119
    Chicken and Broccoli Quiche 86

C

CAKES
    Almond Cake with Raspberry Sauce 214
    Apricot-Lemon Cake 219
    Carrot Cake 218
    Chess Cake 206
    Ellen's Rum Cake 213
    Fudge Cake 206
    Hershey Bar Cake 207

Mama's Buttermilk Cake 204
Other Mama's Prune Cake 210
Red Velvet Cake 209
Sour Cream Coffee Cake 208
Strawberry Cake 220
Candied Sweet Potatoes 112
CANDY
Caramel Candy 234
Fudge Candy 232
Sugared Pecans #2 235
Sugared Walnuts (Pecans) #1 235
Caramel Icing 211
Carrot Cake 218
CASSEROLES
Asparagus Casserole 101
Baked Chicken Salad 146
Baked Onion Casserole 123
Brie Sausage Egg Casserole 88
Chicken Artichoke Casserole 148
Chicken Divan 145
Chicken in Noodles and Wine Sauce 151
Chicken with Pesto Linguini 153
Eggplant Casserole 116
Eggs Vermicelli Casserole 81
Green Bean Casserole 98
Potato Casserole 109
Rice Casserole 93
Sausage Egg Casserole 80
Squash Casserole 104
Tuna Casserole 137
Vegetable Casserole 115
Catharine's Mini BLT's 17
CHEESE
Baked Brie en Croute 5
Becky's Pimento Cheese Sandwiches 37
Betty's Pimento Cheese 38
Bleu Cheese Dressing 76
Brie Sausage Egg Casserole.....88
Cheese Dates, Pecans, or Olives 4
Cheese Dreams 40
Cheese Grits 90
Cheese Soufflé 89
Cheese Straws 4
Cream Cheese Rolls 14
Cream Cheese Olive Nut Sandwiches 36
Ellen's Cheese Spread 18
Individual Cheese Cakes 221
Ham and Swiss Sandwiches 41
Orange Cream Cheese Sweet Rolls 224
Pecan Cream Cheese Sweet Rolls 223
Pineapple Cheese Ball 6
Chess Cake 206
Chess Pie 240
CHICKEN
Baked Chicken and Rice 144
Baked Chicken Salad 146
Chicken Artichoke Casserole 148
Chicken Artichoke Soup 44
Chicken Casserole #1 150
Chicken Casserole #2 152
Chicken Divan.....145
Chicken Gravy 176
Chicken in Noodles and Wine Sauce 151
Chicken Salad 52
Chicken with Pesto Linguini 153
Easy Chicken Tetrazini 149
Grilled Chicken 144

Mama's Fried Chicken 142
Chili 49
Chili Sauce 184
CHOCOLATE
BeBe's Brownies 225
Bobby's Fudge Pie 239
Chocolate Chess Pie 240
Chocolate Éclairs 250
Chocolate Heath Torte ("Stuff") 245
Chocolate Sauce 170
Fudge Cake 206
Fudge Candy 232
Hershey Bar Cake 207
Skillet Chocolate Pie 238
Cobbler 244
Cold Artichoke Spread 9
Congealed Cranberry Salad 56
COOKIES
Crescents 230
Ice Box Cookies 230
Oatmeal Cookies 228
CORN
Corn Light Bread 202
Corn Pudding 102
Fried Corn 103
CORNBREAD (also see Bread)
Cornbread.....192
Cornbread Cakes 196
Cornbread Dressing 194
Cornbread Salad 64
Hot Water Cornbread 196
Mexican Cornbread 201
Spoon Bread 193
Country Fried Steak 158
Covered Cherries 248
CRABMEAT (see also Seafood)
Crab Imperial 130
Miss Polly's Crab Toasts 20
Shrimp and Crab Quiche 87
Cream Cheese Rolls 14
Cream Cheese, Olive, Nut Sandwiches 36
Creole Shrimp 127
Crescents 230
Cucumber Ball 11
Cucumber Sandwiches 35
D
Date Nut Bread 203
DESSERTS
Almond Cake with Raspberry Sauce 214
Almond Ice Box Pie 255
Apricot Fried Pies 254
Apricot-Lemon Cake 219
Banana Pudding 248
BeBe's Brownies 225
Bobby's Fudge Pie 239
Caramel Candy 234
Carrot Cake 218
Chess Cake 206
Chess Pie 240
Chocolate Chess Pie 241
Chocolate Eclairs 249
Chocolate Heath Torte ("Stuff") 245
Cobbler 244
Covered Cherries 248
Ellen's Rum Cake 213
Flan 254
Fudge Cake 206

Fudge Candy 232
Grasshopper Pie 242
Hershey Bar Cake 207
Individual Cheese Cake 221
Jeanne's Lemon Squares 231
Lemon Souffle 250
Mama's Buttermilk Cake 204
Meringue Kisses 246
Other Mama's Prune Cake 210
Pecan Pie 243
Red Velvet Cake 209
Skillet Chocolate Pie ...238
Strawberry Cake 220
Tiramisu 251
Trifle 252
Deviled Oysters 128

DIPS
Broccoli Dip 15
Dip for Vegetables 28
Hot Artichoke Dip 8
K.K.'s Spinach Dip.....12
Layered Nacho Dip 26

DRESSING (See Salad Dressings)

E
Easy Chicken Tetrazini 149
Egg Salad Sandwiches
Eggplant Casserole 116

EGGS
Brie Sausage Egg Casserole.....88
Egg Salad Sandwiches 42
Eggs Vermicelli Casserole 81
Omelet 87
Sausage Egg Casserole 80
Ella's Rolls 197
Ellen's Almond Cake.....214
Ellen's Cheese Spread 18
Ellen's Rum Cake 213
Empanadas.....25
Eye of Round Roast 158

F
Faucon Salad Dressing 68
FISH (also see Seafood)
Grilled Salmon 136
Grilled Yellow Fin Tuna 136
Miss Polly's Fried Fish or Shrimp 132
Tuna Casserole 137
Tuna Marinade 178
Flan 254
French Dressing 77
Fresh Fruit Salad With Poppy Seed Dressing 70
Fresh Limas, Crowder or Black Eyed Peas, Etc. 106
Fried Corn 103
Fried Green Tomatoes 122
Fried Okra 121
FROSTINGS (see Icings)
Frozen Fruit Salad 55
FRUIT
Fresh Fruit with Poppy Seed Dressing 70
Frozen Fruit Salad 55
Fruit Tea 258
Mrs. Brown's Frozen Fruit Salad 58
Fudge Cake 206
Fudge Candy 232

G
Grasshopper Pie 242
GRAVY
Chicken Gravy 176

Green Bean Casserole 98
Green Beans 99
Green Tomato Pickles 188
Grilled Chicken 144
Grilled Salmon 136
Grilled Tarragon Pork Chops 163
Grilled Yellow Fin Tuna 136
Gumbo 48

H
Ham and Swiss Sandwiches 41
Hershey Bar Cake 207
Hollandaise Sauce 172
Homemade Mayonnaise 54
Honey Mustard Dressing 75
HORS d'OEUVRES (see Appetizers)
Hot Artichoke Dip 8
Hot or Cold Asparagus Roll-ups 34
Hot Water Cornbread 196

I
Ice Box Cookies 230
ICINGS
BeBe's Brownies Frosting 225
Betty's Caramel Icing 212
Caramel Icing 211
Chocolate Eclairs Frosting 249
Red Velvet Cake Icing 209
Strawberry Cake Icing 220
Individual Cheese Cakes 221
Instant Hot Tea Mix 260

J
Jane's Caramel Sauce 170
Jean Crawford's Vegetable Salad 59
Jeanne's Lemon Squares 231
Jezebel Sauce 171
Judy's Marinade 177

K
K.K.'s Spinach Dip 12

L
LAMB
Lamb Marinade 179
Leg of Lamb 166
Lasagna 95
Layered Nacho Dip 26
Layered Salad 53
Leg of Lamb 166
LEMON
Apricot-Lemon Cake 219
Jeanne's Lemon Squares 231
Lemon Curd 189
Lemon Soufflé 251

M
Mama's Buttermilk Cake 204
Mama's Fried Chicken 142
Mama's Vegetable Soup 46
Marinade for Pork Tenderloin 175
MARINADES
Judy's Marinade 177
Lamb Marinade 179
Marinade for Pork Tenderloin 175
Tuna Marinade 178
Mary's Mango Salsa 181
Mashed Potatoes 107
Mashed Sweet Potatoes 110
MEAT (also see Beef or Pork)
Baked Ham 165
Bar-b-que Smokies 26
Beef Tenderloin 156

Chili 49
Country Fried Steak 158
Empanadas 25
Eye of Round Roast 158
Grilled Tarragon Pork Chops 163
Ham and Swiss Sandwiches 41
Leg of Lamb 166
Meat Loaf 161
Meat Sauce for Spaghetti or Lasagna 162
Old Time Beef Hash 160
Pork Roast 164
Pork Tenderloin 164
Pull Apart (Pot Roast) 159
Southern Fried Pork Chop 163
Meringue Kisses 246
Mexican Cornbread 201
Mini Ruebens 42
Miss Polly's Crab Toasts 20
Miss Polly's Fried Fish or Shrimp 132
Miss Polly's Shrimp and Grits 134
Miss Polly's Shrimp and Sausage Boil 135
Mozzarella Spread 29
Mrs. Brown's Frozen Fruit Salad 58
MUFFINS
Banana Muffins 217
Sour Cream Muffins 216
MUSHROOM
Mushroom Quiche 86
Toasted Mushroom Sandwiches 39
N
Nut Bread 222
O
Oatmeal Cookies 228
Old Time Beef Hash 160
Omelet 87
Orange Cream Cheese Sweet Rolls 224
Other Mama's Prune Cake 210
P
Pam's Spinach Squares 10
Party Punch 261
PASTA
Betty B's Fettuccine 92
Chicken in Noodles and Wine Sauce 151
Chicken with Pesto Linguini 153
Easy Chicken Tetrazini 149
Lasagna 95
Pasta Salad 60
Risotto with Parmesan 94
Pecan Cream Cheese Sweet Rolls 223
Pecan Pie 243
PICKLES
Green Tomato Pickles 188
Squash Pickles ....., 187
PIES
Almond ice Box Pie 255
Apricot Fried Pie 254
Bobby's Fudge Pie 239
Chess Pie 240
Chocolate Chess Pie 240
Cobbler 244
Grasshopper Pie 242
Pecan Pie 243
Skillet Chocolate Pie 238
Pineapple Cheese Ball 6
PORK (also see Meat)
Baked Ham 165
Grilled Tarragon Pork Chops 163

Pork Roast 164
Pork Tenderloin 164
Southern Fried Pork Chops 163
POTATOES
Candied Sweet Potatoes 112
Mashed Potatoes 107
Mashed Sweet Potatoes 110
Potato Casserole 109
Potato Rolls 199
Potato Salad 62
Twice Baked Potatoes 108
POULTRY (see Chicken)
PRESERVES
Bell Pepper Jelly 186
Strawberry Preserves 189
Pull Apart (Pot Roast).....159
Q
QUICHE
Basic Quiche (Mixture) 82
Chicken and Broccoli 86
Lorraine 84
Mushroom 86
Shrimp and Crab.....87
Spinach 85
R
Ramen Noodle Slaw 66
Red Velvet Cake 209
Remoulade Sauce 180
RICE
Baked Chicken and Rice 144
Rice Casserole 93
Rice Salad 61
Risotto with Parmesan 94
Wild Judy's Rice 91
ROLLS
Cream Cheese Rolls 14
Ella's Rolls 197
Orange Cream Cheese Rolls 224
Pecan Cream Cheese Rolls 223
Potato Rolls 199
Rolls 198
S
SALAD DRESSINGS
Bleu Cheese Dressing 76
Bobby's Quick & Easy Dressing for Fruit 74
Faucon Salad Dressing 68
French Dressing 77
Honey Mustard Dressing 75
Poppy Seed Dressing 70
Sesame Seed Dressing
Spinach Salad Dressing 69
SALAD
Baked Chicken Salad 146
Chicken Salad 52
Congealed Cranberry Salad 56
Cornbread Salad 64
Egg Salad Sandwiches 42
Fresh Fruit Salad 70
Frozen Fruit Salad 55
Jean Crawford's Vegetable Salad 59
Layered Salad 53
Mrs. Brown's Frozen Fruit Salad 58
Pasta Salad 60
Potato Salad 62
Ramen Noodle Slaw 66
Rice Salad 61
Shrimp and Lobster Salad 138

Shrimp Delight 126
Slaw 61
Spinach Salad 69
Tomato Aspic 67
Wilted Lettuce Salad 65
Salmon on a Baguette 21
SANDWICHES
Becky's Pimento Cheese Sandwiches 37
Betty's Pimento Cheese 38
Cheese Dreams 40
Cream Cheese Olive Nut Sandwiches 36
Cucumber Sandwiches 35
Egg Salad Sandwiches 42
Ham and Swiss Sandwiches 41
Hot/Cold Asparagus Roll-ups 34
Mini Ruebens 42
Toasted Mushroom Sandwiches 39
Tomato Sandwiches 32
SAUCES
Chili Sauce 184
Chocolate Sauce 170
Hollandaise Sauce 172
Jane's Carmel Sauce 170
Jezebel Sauce 171
Remoulade Sauce 180
White Sauce 174
Sausage Egg Casserole 80
Sausage Pinwheels 24
SEAFOOD (also see Crab, Fish, or Shrimp)
Bacon Wrapped Water Chestnuts or Shrimp 19
Boiled Shrimp 131
Crab Imperial 130
Creole Shrimp 127
Deviled Oysters 128
Grilled Salmon 136
Grilled Yellow Fin Tuna 136
Gumbo 48
Miss Polly's Crab Toasts 20
Miss Polly's Fried Fish or Shrimp 132
Miss Polly's Shrimp & Grits 134
Miss Polly's Shrimp & Sausage Boil 135
Salmon on a Baguette 21
Seafood in White Wine Sauce 139
Shrimp & Crab Quiche 87
Shrimp & Lobster Salad 138
Shrimp Delight 126
Shrimp Mold 22
Shrimp or Crab Puffs 23
Tuna Casserole 137
Tuna Marinade 178
West Indies Salad 16
Seasoned Oyster Crackers 27
Sesame Seed Dressing 72
SHRIMP (also see Seafood)
Boiled Shrimp 131
Creole Shrimp 127
Miss Polly's Fried Fish or Shrimp 132
Miss Polly's Shrimp & Grits 134
Miss Polly's Shrimp & Sausage Boil 135
Shrimp & Lobster Salad 126
Shrimp Delight 126
Shrimp Mold 22
Shrimp or Crab Puffs 23
Skillet Chocolate Pie 238
Slaw 61
SOUPS
Big C's Gazpacho ...43
Chicken Artichoke Soup 44
Chili 49

Gumbo 48
Mama's Vegetable Soup 46
White Bean Soup 45
Sour Cream Coffee Cake 208
Sour Cream Muffins 216
Southern Fried Pork Chops 163
Spinach Salad and Dressing 69
Spoon Bread 193
Squash Casserole 104
Squash Pickles 187
Stewed Okra 120
Strawberry Cake 220
Strawberry Preserves 189
Sugared Pecans #2 235
Sugared Walnuts (Pecans) #1 235
T
Tiramisu 252
Toasted Mushroom Sandwiches 39
TOMATO
Baked Tomatoes 114
Fried Green Tomatoes 122
Green Tomato Pickles 188
Tomato Aspic 67
Tomato Sandwiches 32
Trifle 253
Tuna Casserole 137
Tuna Marinade 178
Turnip Greens 117
24 Hour Cocktail 261
Twice Baked Potatoes 108
V
Vegetable Casserole 115
VEGETABLES
Asparagus 100
Asparagus Casserole ...101
Baked Apples 114
Baked Beans 120
Baked Onion Casserole 123
Baked Tomatoes 114
Broccoli Ring 119
Candied Sweet Potatoes 112
Corn Pudding 103
Dip for Vegetables 28
Eggplant Casserole 116
Fresh Limas, Crowder or Black Eyed Peas, Etc. 106
Fried Corn 103
Fried Green Tomatoes 122
Fried Okra 121
Green Bean Casserole 98
Green Beans 99
Jean Crawford's Vegetable Salad 59
Mama's Vegetable Soup 46
Mashed Potatoes 107
Mashed Sweet Potatoes 110
Potato Casserole 109
Squash Casserole 104
Stewed Okra 120
Twice Baked Potatoes 108
Turnip Greens 117
Vegetable Casserole 115
White Beans or Black-eyed Peas (from dried) 118
W
West Indies Salad 16
White Bean Soup 45
White Beans or Black-eyed Peas (from dried) 118
White Sauce 174
Wild Judy's Rice 91
Wilted Lettuce Salad 65